GALLOWAY STREET

Growing up Irish in Scotland

John Boyle

BLACK SWAN

GALLOWAY STREET
A BLACK SWAN BOOK : 0 552 99914 8

Originally published in Great Britain by Doubleday,
a division of Transworld Publishers

PRINTING HISTORY
Doubleday edition published 2001
Black Swan edition published 2002

1 3 5 7 9 10 8 6 4 2

Set in 11/13pt Melior by
Phoenix Typesetting, Ilkley, West Yorkshire.

Black Swan Books are published by Transworld Publishers,
61–63 Uxbridge Road, London W5 5SA,
a division of The Random House Group Ltd,
in Australia by Random House Australia (Pty) Ltd,
20 Alfred Street, Milsons Point, Sydney, NSW 2061, Australia,
in New Zealand by Random House New Zealand Ltd,
18 Poland Road, Glenfield, Auckland 10, New Zealand
and in South Africa by Random House (Pty) Ltd,
Endulini, 5a Jubilee Road, Parktown 2193, South Africa.

Printed and bound in Great Britain by
Clays Ltd, St Ives plc.

John Boyle left Scotland at age nineteen and has lived most of his adult life abroad. He taught English in Spain and London, managed language schools in Belgium and Holland, then set up a communication consultancy in Brussels. He now divides his time between Brussels, New York and London, doing commercial voiceovers and writing.

*For Stephanie and Sean
who helped me remember*

'Look how absurd I was when I was young' forestalls cruel criticism but it falsifies history . . . Those emotions were real when we felt them. Why should we be more ashamed of them than of the indifference of old age?

Graham Greene, *A Sort of Life*

Foreword

In the winter of 1993 I went back to Achill Island in the West of Ireland for the funeral of my Aunt Mary. It was a time of some crisis in my life, of confusion and doubt about the way I had chosen to earn a living, about the storm clouds lowering on the horizon of my marriage, about who I was or where I belonged after years of expatriate drift. I was going back to a wild, desolate place that had left its mark on me since I was a boy of ten, when Aunt Mary, returning to Achill after years of exile, had taken me there with her from my home in Scotland for a 'holiday' that was to last an entire summer and one school term.

What was it really that took me back again in 1993?

Aunt Mary was a lifelong spinster who had lived her last years on Achill in willed isolation; the families of her three sisters in Scotland were her closest relatives; it was only right that we be represented at her funeral.

Then there was the question of the will – if there was one. Mary, the sister who had stayed at home to look after their ailing father, Jack Sweeney, had inherited on his death the simple cottage and the narrow strip of land by the sea. There was a long-held understanding among the sisters -- and it had been their father's wish

– that in the event of Mary's death the place should pass to Annie, the youngest of the four and the last to leave home while he was still alive. Yet Mary was notoriously secretive and perverse by nature; there was no knowing what she would do. Given my boyhood link with the cottage in Achill, I confess the thought had sneaked into my mind that she might even have left it to me. In the event, the old woman surpassed herself and wrongfooted all of us by willing everything to none of the above, but to someone quite unexpected.

Mary would have enjoyed the family mayhem that ensued.

As it turned out, I took something altogether different away with me from that trip to Achill.

It seemed that every place I visited, every face I vaguely recalled, stirred memories of the time I had spent there as a boy. Sometimes these memories intruded at awkward moments, never more so than when I rose to read a passage from Scripture during Mary's funeral Mass at Achill Sound. I had made up my mind to do this in my own voice, and not in the actorly tones I adopt for commercial voiceovers, only to falter when I started reading: I was no longer sure what my true voice was. Whatever doubts had surfaced to unsettle me, I came to believe that my reading had been sabotaged, and for good reason, by that ten year old boy.

For years I had been tinkering obsessively with reminiscences about my childhood in Scotland, as if some clue might lie there to my present confusion. It did not help, I began to understand, that these events were being recalled and enhanced by the middle-aged raconteur I had become. Now I felt the need to rediscover – truthfully, without embroidery – the boy I had been.

I found only his ghost, of course, yet he has haunted me ever since. He stands on the sidelines of my life, in the shadows, watchful, reproachful. He knows all my anecdotes; he beats me to the punchlines; he is not impressed. *Cummoan*, he says, *ye know fine there wis mair tae it than that.*

For a long time I persisted, writing this memoir in two distinct voices. Why not? I reasoned. Surely each has his story to tell? The raconteur looking fondly back, recalling a sepia-tinted boyhood across the echoes of the years? And the boy who lived it – insofar as he can remember it truly?

Who's to say where truth ends and fiction begins?

We shape our truths to make them bearable. We take our sad songs and make them better. We grope for meaning. Much of the time we are lost souls whistling in the dark.

But in our hearts we know where truth lies.

Let the boy tell his own story.

Beginnings

I wake up in the night and there's a big dark shape leaning over me. There's a light coming from some-where behind it but all I can see is this shadow above me.

Wheesht, it says. Wheesht now.

I think I can make out a face on it but I can't be sure. The funny thing is I'm not even feart, I just lie there looking up at it and after a while it backs away till all I can see is the dark shape with yellow light around it then the door shuts and everything goes black.

In the morning I'm not sure if this really happened or if it was just me dreaming. So I ask my mammy and she says it was only my daddy come to see me from the Army where he's a soldier in the war. And I know it must be true because he's left me new toys, a painted pirate boat one time made out of wood with real cloth sails strung with twine and another time a wooden horse on wheels, dark brown with big light splashes on its back and a long string for pulling looped through a hole in its muzzle.

That's them Gerry prisoners for ye, says my mammy. Would you be up to them? Making beautiful toys like that out of old lumps of wood that's only fit for

13

throwing on the fire. And they do it for nothin', a wee bit of chocolate your daddy says, or a few Woodbine, that's all they get for it the craitchurs. Ah, them Gerries are the bhoys, I'm telling you. They'll take a bit o' beating, if ye ask me, the same Gerries.

We live in a room in another woman's house, Mammy, Daddy and me and the baby. We are going out somewhere and my daddy is squatting on his hunkers in front of me tying my laces. He's swaying back and forth and this way and that and there's a queer smell about his breath and all at once he staggers back cursing, still on his hunkers, and nearly falls into the fire. Holy Mother o' God, man, my mammy says in her tight whisper, what will Mrs McFadyen think? The baby starts crying and Wheesht, she says to it, Wheesht now, and I'm feart. But my daddy only laughs and though it's a queer laugh and his face looks slack and foolish and not like him I know it's all right and he comes crawling back to tie my lace.

I am riding on my daddy's shoulders. It's dark and there's no-one else. I am holding on tight under his chin because his breath has the queer smell and he's staggering all over the road. He's singing:

> There was a wild colonial boy
> Jack Duggan was his name
> He was born and bred in I-yer-land
> In a place called Castlemaine

Once I hear him muttering 'Mother Machree' and I feel his hands squeezing my ankles and his mouth wet on my knee. I can feel his stubble rasping on the palms

of my hands and the inside of my wrists and his
shoulders swaying and dipping under me.

> *He was his father's only son*
> *His mother's pride and joy*

It is a cold clear night and the sky is riddled with
stars. Beside us is a low flat wall and a pale stretch of
frosty grass then the litup windows of a big square
building, a school, I think.

> *And dearly did his parents love*
> *The wild colonial boy*

One time it's as if he tries to walk along the wall and
he lurches onto the grass and then the world turns
and the litup windows whirl among the stars and I'm
feart I'm going to fall. But he steadies himself and
laughs and mutters, Ye're all right, son, ye're all right,
yer daddy's got ye, don't be afeart, and we're back on
the pavement again and though I'm still feart I'm
excited too, the wild colonial boy riding up there with
his head among the stars.

Galloway Street

1945

Plop.

The pulley up on the ceiling above the table has washing on it that drips down sometimes onto the oilcloth.

You hear one and wait for the next one, but nothing happens for a while so you forget to listen then *Plop*, you hear it again.

Number 4 Galloway Street is where we are now, in a room and kitchen on the top landing. It's always dim in the back room even though it's got a window and a big wardrobe beside it with a long mirror gleaming in the door then there's the big bed where me and Margaret and Frankie sleep.

The kitchen's much brighter with the fire burning in the grate and the big window over the sink. The table with the wet clothes hanging over it is in the middle of the room and on the far wall there's a big bed squeezed into an alcove with thick curtains where my mammy and daddy sleep. Sometimes in the daytime I hide in there and pull the curtains so it's dark and kid on I'm in a tent in the desert or lost in the deep forest at dead of night. There's a fuzzy purple quilt on the bed that feels funny on my fingers like chalk and I get a wee shiver when I touch it. So I always roll it back and play on the bedspread instead because That's candlewick, my mammy says, It has a nicer feel to it.

At the sink the tap is copper and shiny and curved like a swan's neck and you can swing it this way and that and when you run the water not too fast it comes out like glassy rope. I like to stand there making the rope loop sideyways and back again and looking across at the women in their turbans leaning out the windows blethering to each other or shouting down to their weans in the street though when my daddy lifts me up so I can see down there I get dizzy and feart because we're that high up.

When we get back to our close from the shops my mammy lifts me out of the go-chair so she can put the message bag in it instead and drag it up the stone stairs behind us.

squealbump
squealbump
squealbump

Holding on to me with her other hand, up past the lavvies on the half-landings where the bad smells are, drains and pee, past the Deveneys' house on the first landing, and up to the second where she sometimes stops for a rest though she doesn't like to, she says, because we don't know anybody on that landing. Sometimes I trip and I'd fall but for my mammy holding me up.

Arra would ye watch where ye're going?

She's hissing at me because everything echoes dead loud in the close and she doesn't want the neighbours to hear.

17

Haven't I enough to do pulling this go-chair and it full of messages without having to hold you up as well?

So I put out my other hand for balance on the inside wall though I don't like the feel of it, all clammy and sad with wee trickles running down it so you'd think the wall was greetin', and on we go up and up *squealbump squealbump squealbump* till at last there's no more sad wall only railings and daylight because this is the top landing and we're nearly home.

My mammy goes and gets baby Margaret in her big pram back from Mrs Higgins, our neighbour on the landing. Mrs Higgins looks after the baby sometimes. She's a nice woman with gingery hair and specs. Her door is dark shiny wood with a bright brass lock and nameplate and matching letterbox and a fancy doorbell that chimes when you press it. Our door looks brown and scruffy beside it with just the wee nameplate M. BOYLE and scratches round the lock and letterbox and no bell so you have to chap the door.

Arra why would I go paying out money for the like o' that? says my mammy when I ask her. A lot of nonsense is all it is.

But that's not what she says to Mrs Higgins when they're out blethering on the landing.

Isn't that a lovely ring your bell has? she'll say. The Westminster chimes, isn't that what they call it? I might get one like that myself one day, God willing.

1946

Let you be getting up now.

It's freezing cold and the middle of the night and my

mammy's standing beside the bed shaking me by the shoulder.

Wakey wakey, she says. Hallo below. You're going to school today, remember?

It's true. My first day at school. St James's. I get out of bed and do a pee in the po that's kept under the bed. I nearly pee the carpet, I'm shivering that much with the cold. The carpet feels damp under my feet but when I step off it onto the linoleum that's even worse, like stone. My teeth are chattering. We go in the kitchen because she's got the gas cooker lit and the oven door open. She's spread my clean clothes on a chair beside it to heat but it doesn't do much good. My vest and pants are cold and stiff when I put them on. My shirt is even worse, it's like ice, like putting iron armour on your bare skin.

I sit down at the kitchen table. The sky outside is black. I'm still shivering. The oilcloth on the table feels cold and clammy and there's wee puddles where the drips from the pulley have splashed out of the tin basin and pots she keeps there; they're nearly full. She takes them away and wipes the table with a wet cloth and gives me tea and a big plate of porridge with steam coming off it.

That'll warm ye up a bit, she whispers.

We have to be quiet so we don't wake the baby in his cot by her bed or Margaret still sleeping in the big room.

I'm to go on the bus with Porky McNulty from number six, because Patricia his wee sister is in the same class as me. Patricia's her posh name. We call her Rita when we're out playing. She's got a nice face and long wavy hair.

I'm to call Porky by his proper name which is

19

Eugene, my mammy says, or else I'll be in trouble.

Porky, she says, shaking her head. God forgive ye. Did ye ever hear the like?

But Mammy everybody calls him Porky.

Ah well. You're not everybody.

St James's is a big school with thousands of big boys and lassies running about and shouting in the playground. I'm waiting over to the side near the main door steps with the other weans who are there for their first day. Some of the weans standing with their mammies are greetin' but I'm holding it in because of what my mammy said at the bus stop at Caledonia Street.

Ye're a big boy now. Ye're not to be a crybaby.

A tall nun in black robes and hood with a white bib comes out onto the steps. We have to line up in front of her.

Hallo boys and girls, she says. My name is Mother Stanislaus. Welcome to St James's.

Our class teacher is a big stout woman with grey hair tied in a bun. She's not a nun, her name is Miss O'Neill. Her face is old but nice, with double chins.

She smiles at us.

We'll start with something nice and easy, she says. Now. What is a dot? Hands up anybody who knows what a dot is.

Some weans put their hands up and shout, Please Miss! so I put mine up as well. I hope Rita McNulty is looking.

Miss O'Neill asks one after the other but nobody gets it right. Then it's my turn.

Please Miss it's a bump, I say. But that's not right either. I was only guessing. I'm embarrassed but not too much because nobody else gets the answer.

Well, says Miss O'Neill, you can all tell your

mammies and daddies that you learned something on your first day. Because a dot is just . . .

She picks up a stick of chalk and stabs it at the clean blackboard. It makes a wee white spot right in the middle of all the black.

A dot! says Miss O'Neill. That's all it is.

We all look at each other. Right enough, it was dead easy.

1947

Who made you?
   God made me.
Miss O'Neill is teaching us the Catechism. It's a wee blue book full of questions and answers about Our Lord. We've all got our new Catechisms open at the first page.

Mother Stanislaus is standing beside the teacher, watching and smiling. She's only here for today, she says, because the Catechism is so important for our Catholic Faith.

Learn your Catechism, boys and girls, she says. This little book has the answers to all the questions you might have about God and our religion.

Miss O'Neill reads out the questions and we all chant the answers back.

Who made you?
God made me.
Why did God make you?
To know Him love Him and serve Him in this world and to be happy with Him for ever in the next.
In whose image did God make you?
God made me in His own image and likeness.

There's something missing. I put my hand up.

Please Miss!

Yes John, Miss O'Neill says, What is it?

Please Miss, who made God?

Her mouth opens but she doesn't say anything. She looks at Mother Stanislaus. She doesn't say anything either. Then she smiles and so does Miss O'Neill.

Mother Stanislaus comes forward.

Well, John, that's a very clever question and you're a clever boy to ask it. But you see, nobody made God. God made everything. God was always there, before everything else. He is still with us now, and for all eternity. Do you see?

I don't see how God could come from nothing and I don't know what Eternity means but I don't like to say especially after her saying I was clever in front of Rita McNulty. I'm embarrassed because everybody's looking at me.

Yes, Mother.

Miss O'Neill carries on reading out the questions and we all chant the answers.

Where is God?

God is EVERYwhere!

That's the best one because when we say *EVERYwhere!* we're allowed to shout, or near enough, and spread our arms out wide.

When James McGovern spreads his arms out he kids on he's doing a big yawn but Miss O'Neill can't see him because he's hiding behind big Owen Mangan. The boys sitting near him are giggling behind their hands and I'm jealous. I wish I'd thought of that.

But still.

Who made God?

I love Elizabeth McInally. She's in my class at St James's. She's got a nice quiet face with a soft mouth and fair wavy hair and she lives in Blythswood Terrace near the Fountain Gardens. It's dead posh there, the tenements are red stone not dark and sooty like Galloway Street. I think she loves me back, that's what Helen Murray told me and she's her best pal. The happiest day of my life was Pat Foley's birthday party when we played Postman's Knock and I kissed Elizabeth McInally. When I tasted her mouth I was that dizzy I thought I was fainting. I wanted to kiss her again but they started a new game.

I watch Elizabeth in the classroom sometimes, though I kid on I'm just looking at the pictures up on the wall. There's one I like called Rockabye Baby, a wee baby in its cradle high up in the branches of a tree. There's a rhyme:

> *Rockabye baby in the treetops*
> *When the wind blows the cradle will rock.*

I always feel sorry for the baby, stuck up in a tree all by itself. The picture is near where Elizabeth sits and when I look at them it makes me happy and sad at the same time.

> *When the bough breaks the cradle will fall*
> *Down will come cradle, baby and all.*

Sometimes she can feel me watching her. A funny look comes over her face and she turns her head dead slow and sees me. Then she smiles at me. A wee shy smile. It's a secret between Elizabeth and me.

I dream it's playtime and all the weans are out in the

playground when suddenly I come galloping in on a big white horse like Roy Rogers and Trigger at the Astoria. I'm wearing a big white hat like Roy's and a red bandanna. They all stop and stare at me, they can't believe their eyes. When I get to Elizabeth I reach down dead gallant and scoop her up into the saddle in front of me. Then Trigger rears up and whinnies and paws the air, I pull the reins round and we gallop away in a big cloud of dust and leave St James's behind for ever.

We're playing a game in the old washhouse out the back of number six, me and Rita McNulty and Agnes Brown and Rita's wee brother, Wee Johnny. The lassies are the mammies making the tea for the daddies coming in from their work. They've got this old pot out of the midden and they're trying to put water in it by scraping it sideways through puddles but that doesn't work. Then Wee Johnny says, Hey wait a minute, and he takes out his wullie and pees in the pot. The lassies start giggling, but it's OK because Wee Johnny is Rita's wee brother and he's only four. They get very interested in how much he can pee and how the steam rises off it. They put the half-full pot on two bricks and that's the cooker. Not long after that they're looking for more water to make more tea and Wee Johnny's got no pee left so Rita McNulty comes up to me and says, Right, mister, we need mair watter for the kettle. So I unbutton my trousers and out comes my wullie and Rita smiles at me and says, That's fine, and nice and hoat, tae. Ye can turn the tap aff noo. And we sit on bricks stood on end and curl our fingers dead posh as if we're holding china cups and kid on we're mammies and daddies having their tea.

After a while I hear my mammy shouting for me.

John? John? Are ye there? she's shouting out the landing window at number four and at first I'm worried I'm going to get a row. But no, she's smiling away and waving at me to come up to the house. Whit's it fur? I shout up to her. But she only smiles and waves. Just come up, she says, I have somethin' to show ye.

So up I go.

When I get there the door's half open but the lobby's empty as if there's nobody in. My mammy must be hiding. I look round laughing, wondering what game she's playing and what she has to show me, and out she comes from behind the door with a funny wee tight smile on her face. Oh, there ye are. And she shuts the door and hits me a skelp on the back of the head that scatters me on the floor. God forgive ye, she's hissing at me, in the tight voice she has for shouting at us so the neighbours on the landing won't hear her, Ye're filthy. Taking your trousers down and making a show of yerself for all the world to see. In front of wee girls too, and you a Catholic boy. Have ye no shame at all? Holy Mother o' God we're disgraced at ye.

WhydidGodmakeyou?

She's trying to hit me where I am on the floor but she's a stout woman and not able to bend down easily and I'm crawling away as fast as I can to hide under the big bed in the kitchen, so she grabs the brush from its corner and stabs at my back with the bristly head of it and gets in a couple of good kicks in my side with her woolly slippers before I crawl under the bed and lie there bawling in the stoury dark with my heart choking me because I'm a disgrace to the world and I've driven my mammy mad.

*   *   *

25

Miss O'Neill keeps a wee box on her desk for the Black Babies.

If you have a penny to spare, boys and girls, she says, Put it in the box and it will go to help the black babies.

The black babies live in Africa. They're very poor and they don't get enough to eat. And they haven't got proper schools to go to, like St James's.

They're not as lucky as you, says Miss O'Neill. And you can stop making faces, James McGovern, it's not funny.

She says the White Fathers go to darkest Africa to convert the Pagan. Pagans don't believe in Our Lord. And that's the worst thing of all about the black babies. They haven't been baptized. It's not their fault, they don't know any better, but they can never go to heaven. They go to Limbo.

When I think about all the black babies lying there in Limbo for ever and ever and never seeing Our Lord it makes me sad. I'd like to put a penny in Miss O'Neill's box every week. But when I ask my mammy she flies into a temper.

Arra where does she think we're going to get pennies to give them? God knows I pity the craitchurs, but you can tell Miss O'Neill we have babies of our own to feed.

I'm ashamed when she says these things. Thank God Miss O'Neill can't hear her. Still, once in a blue moon I get a penny because if I never put anything in the box, she says, they'll be talking about us and we'll be shamed altogether.

When you put enough pennies in, you can name a black baby. I'm going to call mine Richard, after Richard the Lionheart. James McGovern says he wants to call his Geronimo, but I tell him it has to be a Christian name.

He never puts pennies in the box anyway.

I imagine my black baby, wee Richard, sitting at his desk in Africa in a spotless white shirt, listening to the White Father. I wonder if he ever thinks about the boy who saved him, the boy from St James's School, in faraway Scotland?

If I meet him one day, will he know it's me?

The only visitors we get in Galloway Street are relations, except when Mrs Higgins on our landing or one of the Deveneys from down the stairs comes to the door for the lend of a cup of milk or sugar or to change a shilling for the meter. But they're not real visitors so they don't count. Most of our relations are not real relations either, though my mammy says it comes to the same thing.

Aren't they Irish, God help us, no more than ourselves?

There's my Uncle John who's my daddy's real brother though you'd never think it to look at him, a big man with buck teeth who's got a cushy job up in Riccartsbar Asylum. He tells us great yarns about the loonies and the daft antics they get up to and he likes to sing old Irish songs especially when he has a whisky in him. *Hallo Patsy Fagan you're the apple of my eye*, he sings, or *I met her in the garden where the praities grow*.

The funny thing is, my Uncle John's got a terrible stutter. Hallo Ma-Mick, he says to my daddy when he comes in, and Hallo Ma-Maggie to my mammy. But he never stutters when he's singing. Maybe that's why he likes singing so much.

The grownups all tap their feet and clap and say, Good on ye, John! He sings 'The Homes of Donegal' and they start wiping their eyes. He sings 'The Mountains of Mourne Sweep Down to the Sea'. He sings till they start taking wee fly keeks at the clock and saying The Lord save us, is that the time already?

My Uncle John lives in the prefabs with old Jimmy Bradley and Missis Bradley. They're not his real mammy and daddy but that's another story, my mammy says. I still have to call them Uncle Jimmy and Auntie Bradley.

My Uncle John is big and stout and tall, six foot four, he says. My daddy looks dead wee and skinny beside him.

I'm five foot eight, he says and he always straightens himself up when he says it. Same heighth as yer mammy.

Heighth. That's how he says it.

But anybody can see she's a bit taller, even when she's only wearing slippers on her feet.

My daddy's mammy died in Donegal when the two boys were still wee weans and my grandpa Boyle couldn't bring them up on his own and it was fixed up that one of them was to be adopted by the Bradleys in Scotland. So they took John, the eldest, and left wee Mick behind in Donegal with his old man.

An' a hard life Ah had of it too, he's always telling us. Out of school by the time I was twelve and up at six every morning to help the old man in the field.

Ah well, it's too bad about ye, man dear, says my mammy. But would ye be up to them Bradleys? How well they took the big healthy one?

I get the feeling she doesn't like the Bradleys that much.

One time she hints that my Uncle John is only my daddy's half-brother though it seems to me it should be

28

the other way round. But when I ask her about it all she says is, Never you mind.

It's a mystery.

And then there's my Auntie Margaret who's not really my auntie, just my mammy's second cousin from Achill. She's a nicelooking lady with a lovely smile and a comfy chest and her married name is Mrs Young. Her man is Jimmy Young but he never comes near us because he's a Protestant.

Barney Molloy is a big dark man from Donegal with a wee tash on his lip who's a labourer like my daddy and sometimes they work together digging roads and building houses. He never takes a drink, only a cup of tea with plenty sugar, and he never says much.

Ah but he thinks a lot, the same Barney, my mammy says.

No flies on Barney, believe you me.

His wife is Mrs Molloy and she's a wee skinny woman with a pale face and coalblack eyes with dark rings round them. She just sits there and stares and never a word out of her.

Nobody ever says her first name, even Barney calls her Mrs Molloy.

Most of the time the visitors just turn up on our doorstep. I don't think we're ever expecting them because my mammy always flies into a panic when she hears them chapping the door.

Quick, she hisses at us. Pick up the papers, quick, hurry up. Put them toys and things out of sight. Oh Jesus Mary and Joseph look at the state of this house.

The way she says it you'd think she's nearly greetin'. We all have to rush about picking up wee bits of paper and fluff off the carpet and cramming clothes and toys into the drawers.

29

Then it's Well, is one o' ye going to open that door, or what's the matter wit' ye at all? Are ye sleepin' or what?

She says this in her normal voice, out loud so the visitors will hear her. Hoping they'll think it was just us weans that forgot to open the door.

Well hallo, she says when the door is open at last, and they're standing there on the landing in their good visiting clothes.

Come in, come in. Ye're welcome. The house is upside down, but come in anyway, take your coats off, sit yerselves down.

Arra don't be silly, they say. Sure the house is grand.

They all sit round the fire with cups of tea and buns or biscuits and talk about Home.

Home means Ireland. My mammy even calls it that when she's sitting there at our own fireside.

I had a letter from Home last week, she'll say, or Have you any news from Home?

She's always hoping for news of Poor Pat that I've never seen. My mammy's got three sisters, my Auntie Bridget, Mary and Annie and Poor Pat is their brother who went missing years ago. Nobody knows where he is, or if he's alive or dead, but there's always rumours about him. Some say he's in America, doing well for himself, running a big public house. Or he's down in England somewhere, on the building sites.

I have a notion he's on the ships, Old Jimmy Bradley was saying one time. Sailing the seas, that's where he'll be.

That's my favourite. I like to think of my mysterious Uncle Pat on the deck of a big ship, in his seaman's gansey, staring at the far horizon. I've only got three uncles and it's a bit sad that there's one I've never even seen, so I'm hoping he comes home one day.

Wherever home is.

If Ireland is Home, I wonder, what about this place? What about Galloway Street and Scotland? Do they not count?

When I ask my mammy she only laughs.

Ah it's just habit, *ahashki*. Force of habit, as the one said.

But Scotland's hame noo, intit?

Yes, it is. Paisley. Paisley, Scotland. That's my home now.

She says it as if she's testing to see what it sounds like. But it makes no difference. Home means Achill.

To hear them talking Achill is a great place and so is Donegal where my daddy grew up. Barney Molloy comes from there as well. There's fairies and ghosts in Ireland, and haunted houses and banshees. The banshee is my favourite.

The name makes me think of the ghosts you get in the *Beano* and the *Dandy*, a white sheet shaped like a head and shoulders with empty eyes and a long floaty tail, and nothing inside only an evil spirit. When the banshee is seen near somebody's house, you know that person is going to die. Sometimes you don't even see the banshee, you only hear it moaning and howling in the night.

The one that tells us about the banshee is Old Jimmy Bradley. He used to be a nightwatchman on the railways. I picture him sitting up all night staring into the dark with just a wee fire for company. That's probably how he knows.

But whether you see it or whether you hear it, says Old Jimmy Bradley, taking his pipe out of his mouth, damn the bit of difference does it make for it means you're a dead man, and that's as sure as I'm sitting here tonight.

He sits there nodding heavy and slow with his hands on his knees and the women make the sign of the Cross and mutter The Lord bless us and save us and keep us from harm and for a while you'd swear the heat had gone out of the fire. Everybody goes dead quiet and I wonder if they're all like me, thinking about the banshee out there in the dark, hovering, waiting.

Babies come from hospitals. Mammies have to go there to buy them. I came from Barshaw Park hospital.

So, my mammy says, If somebody ever asks you were you born in a park, you can say Yes.

Whit wid they ask me that fur?

It's a joke, *ahashki*. It's what people say if you walk out the door and leave it wide open behind you. Were you born in a park? Meaning, a place with no doors. Well you can say, Yes as a matter of fact I was. Because you were. D'ye see? That'll put them in their place.

She's telling me all this because she's going to the hospital soon to get a new baby. I don't see why we need one, because we've got me and Margaret and Frankie already and that's plenty, but my mammy says she might get a wee sister for Margaret this time.

Mammy, I ask her, how much wis ah?

What?

How much did ye hiv tae pay for me? In Barshaw Park?

Oh. Tuppence.

That's no' very dear, is it?

No *ahashki*, it is not. Ye were cheap. A bargain.

Will the new baby be tuppence as well?

Oh, a bit dearer maybe. Prices are going up all the time nowadays.

She says that's enough questions, she's worn out at us.

Nowadays. I like that word.

She has to stay in the hospital for a few days to make sure she likes the new baby before she brings it home. My daddy's going to look after us when she's away. He's done it before, one time my mammy was sick.

It's good when he does it.

Are yiz gettin' enough grub? he keeps asking us when she's away in hospital. Am Ah lookin' after yiz all right?

Better than ma mammy, he's hoping we'll say. It's nearly true as well, because he always gives us extra grub at dinnertime, though he's not as good at cooking.

Except chips. He's great at chips. My mammy hardly ever makes us chips.

After all that, when she comes back from the hospital there's no new baby with her. She's sick. She has to stay in her bed.

We're wondering what happened.

Are babies too dear nowadays? I ask my daddy.

Arra don't be botherin' me wi' yer questions, he says. Can ye no' see yer mammy's sick? She's too sick to be looking after another baby an' that's all about it. God knows we have our hands full wi' the three of ye.

He's beginning to talk like my mammy. I think he's getting fed up looking after us on his own.

Away ye go now and don't be botherin' me, all right son?

His voice has gone quiet all of a sudden and he gives me a pat on the head, I don't know what for.

He's stopped making us chips. All we get nowadays is pieces 'n cheese.

He tells us jokes he hears at his work. They're always about Pat and Mick.

Pat and Mick are building a house. Mick's up on the scaffold laying bricks and Pat's down below plastering inside the house. Suddenly Mick drops a brick.

— Look out below! he shouts. So poor Pat looks out the window . . . D'ye get it? *Looks out!* . . . and bedamt if the brick doesn't hit him a clout on the head!

My daddy's laughing that much we can hardly hear the end. My mammy sits there shaking her head and tutting.

That's terrible, she says. Always making poor Pat out to be stupid. Any excuse at all to have a laugh at the poor old Irishman.

Arra what's the matter wit' ye? says my daddy. Wasn't it an Irishman that told us it, big Mick Flaherty the gangerman? Can ye no' take a joke or what? I wouldn' mind but ye're laughin' yerself.

It's true. She's smiling. She can't help it.

Whit'll we talk aboot, eh?

This is what my wee brother whispers in my ear at night when he's feart of the dark. To tell the truth I'm a bit feart myself even though there's three of us in the big bed in the back room, me on the outside because I'm the oldest and Margaret by the wall because she's a lassie and the next oldest and wee Frankie in the middle.

I don't know if Margaret is feart of the dark because she usually goes to sleep quite fast so she doesn't say much. She's in a wee world of her own over there by the wall. But I know Frankie is because he's always telling me, though of course I can never tell him back in case he thinks his big brother is a big softie.

I don't know what's worse, lying there with my eyes open or shut. If I keep them open I see the room all dark and different, with shapes moving in the shadows near the curtains or misty in the wardrobe mirror, like in the horror pictures at the Bug Hut. When the light is still on in the kitchen it's like fire burning the edges of the door and blazing through the keyhole. It's worse when it gets switched off. That's when I know the zombie behind the door will come to get me. I'm sure it's a zombie even though I should know it's just a big pile of old coats hanging on the hook. Then I'm feart to shut my eyes in case it jumps on me when I'm not looking. Everything goes dead quiet at night and you hear all these things you never notice during the day, the way the floor or the furniture creaks for no reason and the wind rattles the panes and makes the curtains move and batwing shadows flit on the ceiling where the light spills through from the lamppost down below. And sometimes a long goods train goes rumbling past at the dead end of Galloway Street and makes the whole house shudder and its long lonely whistle is like the howl of the banshee.

So me and Frankie lie there every night trying not to think about the ghosts and vampires creeping all round us in the shadows or under the bed.

After a while Frankie gives me a wee dunt.

Whit'll we talk aboot the night, eh?

Sometimes it's me that asks him first: Whit d'ye want tae talk aboot?

I say it that way on purpose so he'll not know I'm feart as well, he'll think it's just me being good to him because I'm his big brother. It's a wee trick the two of us have to keep our minds off the dark when we're trying to get to sleep. We lie there and talk about football or playing bools or fighting or something that happened at school, anything at all to cheer us up and keep us going until our eyes start to shut or our feet start to slip that sudden way they do so you think you're falling off the edge of a cliff but no, it's all right, you're only falling into sleep. Sometimes one of us nods off a bit too early and then the other one has to cough out loud or give him a dunt and whisper in his ear to wake him back up.

Are ye sleepin' yet?

It's dead annoying if you're the one that went to sleep first, but you put up with it because you know the next time it could be you that's lying there all on your own in the dark, surrounded by shadows of God knows what.

Sometimes that's what happens, Margaret and Frankie snoring away and me left by myself wide awake and staring at the ceiling. There ye are and the boat away, as my mammy would say. This is the only time I say my prayers, but not the way you're supposed to, before you even get into bed, kneeling down at the foot of it like Christopher Robin. I lie there curled up under the bedclothes and pray to God and hope to God He doesn't know it's only because I'm feart and I've got nobody else to talk to. And even if He does, because God is all-knowing, I hope He'll forgive me because God is all-merciful as well.

What I'm praying is that no ghosts will appear to me in the night, even if it's somebody I know and they mean me no harm. The only dead people I know are my granny Boyle who died when my daddy was a wee boy back in Donegal and my granny Sweeney who died on Achill Island when my mammy was a young girl.

And a hard life they had of it too, *ahashki*, my mammy says. But they're gone now, God rest them.

And she sighs and shakes her head the way she does.

Of course I don't know my two grannies at all, I've never even seen their photos, but you never know, they might want to come back and visit their grandson. I picture two faded old ashgrey women in black shawls standing at the end of the bed looking down at the three of us and shaking their heads and sighing, *Ahashki, ahashki.*

Then they fade away.

I don't know what *ahashki* means, but I'm sure that's what they'd say. My mammy says it all the time.

I don't want a visit from my Guardian Angel, either. I'm glad he's up in heaven looking after me but I don't want to see him down here on earth especially not in the middle of the night. Hardly a day goes by at St James's without Mother Agnes or Mother Bernadette telling us about some holy person being visited in the night by an Angel of the Lord. The man gets wakened up by this brilliant light at the foot of the bed and there in the middle of the light is the Angel, with the long blond hair and the shiny wings. And the Angel always says the same thing.

Be not afraid.

It's all right for him to talk, but I always feel sorry for the poor soul who gets woken up in the dark by this apparition. It's a wonder they don't die of heart failure; I think I would. But no, according to Mother Bernadette and Mother Agnes, the Angel just goes ahead and delivers the message or the summons and the holy person is always happy to be whisked away

37

to sit at the right hand of the Lord for all eternity.

So they say anyway.

I wonder how they know.

One way or the other, it seems there's a fair chance I might be called in the night and that's another reason I say my prayers, so at least my soul will be in a state of grace when I die. But I still want to make a good impression when my mammy and daddy find my body in the morning, so I take a bit of trouble to get myself ready. I comb my hair in a nice shed with my fingers and try to breathe through my nose with my mouth shut, because my mammy's always telling me I look like an amathon with my mouth open. Then I lie there on my back with my hands crossed on my breast that holy way the saints do it. I can picture my mammy and daddy in the morning when they find me stretched out dead in the bed, and how sad they'll be that I'm gone, though they'll be proud as well when they realize what a holy person their eldest son was, even if it's too late.

Then I'll be called Saint John of Galloway Street, maybe, or Blessed John Boyle at least, like Blessed John Bosco, because it always takes ages before the Church recognizes you as a saint, no matter how holy you are when you die.

Dadarah dadarah dadarah,
  Balloons for woollen rags!

That's the ragman blowing his bugle and shouting in the street. I look out the kitchen window and down and I see his cart outside number ten, a flat cart heaped high with old clothes and junk, and he's holding up long thin sticks in each hand with bright balloons tied onto them like flags, red and yellow and blue and green, some fat and round and others long and pointy or twisty, and his big old Clydesdale horse just stands there with its head bent in its nosebag munching. Sometimes after a while it lifts up its tail and does a number two out there in the street, a big pile of keich with steam coming off it and a bad smell and all the weans gather round it laughing and pointing. The ragman just shovels sand on it from a big iron pail he keeps on the cart and after a couple of days it gets all dried up and doesn't smell that bad, you can even pick the lumps up and throw them like snowballs. When they hit you they burst and smash to brown powder on your clothes and then the bad smell comes back strong.

I stand there watching the weans running out of their closes with wee bundles of rags then running back laughing and waving their new balloons, but when I want to go out and get one and I ask my mammy if we've got any rags she only says, If we have itself we're keeping them and not giving them away for a few oul' balloons. Sure what are they anyway only a lot of nonsense and a waste of money and wouldn't you be better off asking him if he'd give us some of them oul' clothes he has below on his cart because God knows there's good wear in them yet.

When she says this I don't even want to go outside in case my pals hear my mother talking like this and putting me to shame. So I stay there at the window footering with the copper tap on the sink that's shaped like a swan's neck and watching till the ragman backs his horse out into the road and gets up on the cart and taps the horse with the whip.

Gerrup, he says to it, and clucks his tongue twice.

And I'm still watching as the old horse heaves and the cartwheels squeal and they creak away slow down the street with the big iron hoofs going *clop clop*

clop and sparking on the cobbles and all the weans skipping along behind them shouting and waving their balloons.

1948

I'm joining the library because you can when you're seven. I go up the broad stone steps to the big grey building in the high street with tall columns like you see in pictures at school about the Romans, and high narrow doors in dark wood with glass panels and I can hardly believe they'll let me in. But I show my card to a poshlooking lady in a navy cardigan and pearls and a wavy perm who's standing at the desk and she just smiles and says All right sonny, in ye go. Inside it's all warm and dead quiet with tall wood shelves stacked with hundreds of books, maybe thousands. The floor is this polished wood that shines like glass and I wonder am I really allowed to walk across it in and out the shelves and pick out any book that takes my fancy?

At first I'm feart to even touch the books and I just wander about trying to look as if I'm used to being in a posh place like this and jumping whenever the floorboards squeak under my feet because there's big signs saying SILENCE and I get the feeling everybody's looking at me. At last I pick out a book because I like the title, *Watcher of the Night*. It makes me think of Old Jimmy Bradley on the railways, sitting by his wee fire at night watching the moonshine on the tracks. Or me lying awake in the dark. The words are printed over a dark picture on the cover, two huge eyes staring out of the dark at me, scary and mysterious. Like the banshee. It's a book about owls with a lot of glossy black and white photos and great drawings. I don't know anything about owls but I'm that excited I want to take it. I can't believe I can just walk up to the counter and the posh lady will let me take this fancy book away home with me to 4 Galloway Street, because if she could see where it was going she might change her mind. But no, she just slides a wee ticket out and stamps the book inside with a big chrome stamp machine then hands it back to me and smiles. I go out the door and down the steps with the book under my arm and I'm that excited I'm shaking. It feels as though I'm stealing this book.

But nobody shouts, or runs after me, or stops me.

The bully of Galloway Street is Drummond Love. The Lord save us, my mammy says whenever she hears us talking about him. What kind of a name is that? She's right, too: it's a grim, Scottish, Protestant kind of a name, grimmer even than Stuart Cunningham or Morton McGrory because the first name isn't a Christian name. Drummond, with a kinda drumroll on the R. And somehow after that Love doesn't sound much like the love we hear about at the Astoria or the Picture House, where the cowboy always kisses the lady at the end, or the love of God we read about in the Catechism. It seems to me that the Catholics in our street have softer, friendlier names, like Patricia McNulty in the next close and her big brothers Ainas and Eugene, or Wullie and Danny Deveney in our close. Except for Charlie Miller at number eight. Miller's a Protestant name but Charlie's a Catholic the same as us. Even our school, St James's, has a nicer sound to it than theirs. They go to the North School, a place as black and stony as it sounds.

There is a kind of a dread about the name Drummond Love, though I don't know if that's just the sound of it or Drummond Love himself. He's bigger than any other boy in the street, with these dead, staring eyes and thick lips, and he keeps himself to himself. Nobody really likes him though McGrory and Cunningham let on they do. They keep in with him because they're scared of him and they know everybody else is. If you get into an argument with them they'll sometimes shout Ah'll get Drummond Love oantae you! and you go about for days after in agony for fear they meant it.

One day my pal Wullie Deveney comes into our close howling, the blood pouring from his nose. Drummond Love hit me, he's shouting, running up the stairs to his house. Nobody says anything, because if Drummond Love hits you there's nothing to be done. But a few minutes later Wullie comes back down, still sniffling, the blood and tears scrubbed from his face, dabbing his nose with a hanky.

Ma daddy says I've tae fight Drummond Love, he says, and we stare at him. Nobody can fight Drummond Love. But it turns out Mr Deveney has told Wullie that if he doesn't go back out and fight Drummond Love he'll give Wullie a hammering himself and Wullie is more feart of his daddy than he is of Drummond Love.

Mr Deveney is famous in Galloway Street. He's a big quiet man who keeps himself to himself and one day he fought a man from Brown's Place across Underwood Road because of something bad he said about the Pope. The man must have been a Rangers supporter, a Bluenose as we call them behind their backs. When Mr Deveney walked over to the swing park at Brown's Place that day it felt like every man and boy from Galloway Street, and some of the women too, followed him to watch the fight. I was away at the back with the other weans and we couldn't see much, but we heard all the roars and the thud of the punches and the grunts so it was nearly as good. Then there was a hush and the crowd broke up and Mr Deveney came out stripped to the waist with his face all puffy and bruised and his white thick body streaked with blood, and we knew he'd won from what the men around him were saying.

Good man yerself, Pat.

That'll shut his big mouth for a while.

That'll show them.

And now Wullie Deveney is going to fight Drummond Love. We walk along beside him and word gets round the street and soon boys are coming out of the closes on all sides and walking around us and behind us, jostling and asking questions.

Hey Deveney, Morton McGrory shouts, when he hears. You're mad, so y'are. Drummond Love'll kill ye.

Wullie doesn't say anything back, just keeps walking with his mouth set tight and I think, He's really gonnae do it.

When we get to Galbraith's corner there's a gang of boys there waiting and Drummond Love is among them. He has an awkward look about him as if he can't believe that a wee smout like Wullie Deveney is going to take him on.

But when we get there that's what Wullie does. He just keeps walking right up to him and everybody is waiting to hear what he'll say, but he doesn't say a word only draws back his fist and punches Drummond Love in the mouth. And Drummond Love is that

amazed he wipes his hand across his cut lip and looks
at the blood and while he's doing that Wullie thumps
him in the ear and the fight is on. And though
Drummond Love is much bigger and harder than
Wullie and soon there's blood all over Wullie's face
and spattered on his shirt, we can see Wullie is never
going to give in, and we know it's because he's feart of
his daddy but Drummond Love doesn't know that.
You can see he's embarrassed fighting a wee boy like
Wullie and wondering what else he has to do to make
him stop. And then Mrs Mackenzie from number three
and Mrs Gilmour from number five lean out of their
windows shouting, That's terrible, 's a disgrace so it is,
we're phonin' for the polis, yeez better get away hame
before they catch ye.

We know they don't mean it because we don't see
anybody running up to the phone box on Underwood
Road, but nobody wants the polis coming round. So
somebody shouts it's a draw and they should shake
hands like they do in the pictures and that's what they
end up doing. But when we walk back beside Wullie
we're like the men who walked beside Mr Deveney,
because in a way he won. And maybe Drummond Love
thinks the same, because when I look back he's
standing there in front of Galbraith's window with his
pals all round him but from the look on his face you'd
think he's all by himself and for once in my life I
nearly feel sorry for Drummond Love.

There's news from Home.

We're in the kitchen this day and there's a heavy
step outside on the landing, then three heavy knocks at
the door.

My mammy turns round from the sink and looks at

my daddy then at me. Her face has gone white.

The Lord save us, she says, trying to make a joke of it. What kind o' a knock is that?

She starts drying her hands on her apron.

That's a polisman's knock, my daddy says, if ever Ah heard wan.

He looks worried as well.

He goes and opens the door and sure enough I can see a big bobby out there in his uniform. The two of them stand muttering for a while in the lobby then my daddy shuts the door and comes back in.

He's holding up a wee yellow envelope.

It's oney a telegram, he says, smiling.

He holds it out to my mammy.

Telegram for Margaret Boyle. That's what the man said.

She's not smiling. She's still white in the face.

Oh Jesus Mary and Joseph, she says. It's Pat. Poor Pat. Something's happened.

She sits down and opens the telegram and starts reading it. We watch her. She reads it again. She just sits there.

It's scary to watch her.

What is it, in the name o' God? my daddy says.

It's from Mary, at Home. It's my father, God rest him. He's gone. God have mercy on us.

Her father's Jack Sweeney. She's told us how in Achill the children got nicknames because there were too many with the same last name. Too many Sweeneys and Corrigans and Cooneys and Fadyens. So my mammy was called Maggie Jack, after her father, and her sisters were Bridgie Jack, Mary Jack and Annie Jack.

I suppose Poor Pat must have been Paddy Jack.

It wouldn't work in Paisley, mind. I'd be Johnny Maggie, Margaret would be Maggie Mick. It would sound daft.

I've never seen my grandpa Jack Sweeney, not even his photo. But she's told us how he'd be back and forth to America, to Boston, getting work and sending money back to Achill. And the yarns he'd tell. About the Achill man that went over there one time, Big Seamus Somebody, and he couldn't get a job, he was that thick and slow, so he was back home on the next boat. And begod he'd have the ears worn out on ye for ever after, listenin' to him givin' out about his days travelling the world.

Many's the time I was over beyond in Ameriky, Big Seamus would say. Ah yiss, yiss. An' I walked down Broadway too!

He asked my grandpa Jack to write a letter for him one time and he started off: *Dear Surr, A letter at ye . . .* God save the mark, the poor fella couldn't write, ye see, my mammy tells us, and he thought that was how the educated ones would begin a letter.

Dear Surr, a letter at ye, she'll say again. Ah, may God forgive us for laughin' . . .

We all laugh when we hear this story, except my daddy. He just smiles that shy way he has and shakes his head. I don't think it's that funny either, to tell you the truth, but you have to laugh when you see my mammy laughing. She's a big stout woman and her whole chest heaves and quakes when she laughs and the tears come rolling down her cheeks.

She's not laughing now.

But she's not greetin' either. She sits there holding the telegram in her lap and looking into the fire.

46

Are ye all right? my daddy says. Will Ah make ye a wee cup o' tea?

She shakes her head. Ah, sure what's the use? He's gone now. God rest him, and there's nothing we can do about it. Not a thing, *ahashki*. That's the way o' the world, sure.

She folds the telegram and puts it in her apron pocket and gets up and goes back to her washing at the sink.

My daddy's watching her. He can hardly believe she's not greetin' and her father dead.

He jerks his head back and tuts and sighs that hopeless way he has and sits looking into the fire, shaking his head.

He's the one that's nearly greetin'.

I don't like school dinners much. It's nearly always totties 'n mince, anyway, though not like we get at home. School dinner totties are mashed, they're spread out all pale and lumpy in a big steel tray so the dinner woman can just scoop a big daud onto your plate and the mince is this brown gravy she slops over the top that's that lumpy and runny it would scunner you just to look at it. It puts me in mind of diarrhoea, to tell the truth, and I have to make myself think of something else before I can eat it. I don't like cabbage or leeks either, especially cabbage because it smells rotten, like when my mammy is steeping sweaty socks and pants in the basin.

But even totties 'n mince or cabbage is not as bad as when we get sago for pudding. I hate sago that much I nearly feel sick when I hear the word, especially when I'm standing there in the dinner queue waiting.

Sago the day! says Fatty McKee, and you'd think it

was chocolate and ice cream, he sounds that pleased. But I can feel my stomach sinking and my head going giddy at the thought of it. Sago is like rice only it's this whitey grey stuff with wee blobs in it you can nearly see through, like the frogspawn you get down the Mill pond, all joogly and shivery. And as if that wasn't bad enough, they put a big splodge of raspberry or black-currant jam in it, right in the middle.

It's no use trying to explain this to Mother Agnes, the wee nun in charge, when she scolds me for not eating my sago, or my cabbage or my macaroni cheese.

Offer it up, is all she says. Offer it up!

Offer it up. She always says that. It means you're not to complain, you're to offer your suffering up to God. But I'm sure God wouldn't thank me for a plate of joogly sago.

Some of the boys love sago and they churn it up with their spoons so the colour of the jam runs into the sago and turns it red or purple. James McGovern knows I hate sago and sometimes he sits across from me and stirs his up on purpose just to scunner me. Then he starts slurping it up with his spoon, making horrible sookin' noises and rubbing his belly after each spoonful.

Yum yum, he says. Yumyumyum.

He licks his lips so I can see the purply mess on his tongue.

Fatty McKee eats his much the same way but he doesn't mean any harm by it, it's just because he likes sago. Anyway Fatty's always in too much of a hurry to waste any time in the canteen; he's great at football, he's bound to play for Celtic when he grows up, and he can hardly wait to get out to the playground. Sometimes he's in that much of a hurry he'll shove

48

wee bits of dinner or pudding in his jacket pocket for after and rush out to get in the game. He's a great dribbler and he likes to play out on the wing and sometimes you'll see him dribbling the ball towards you and eating a big daud of tart or cake out of his jacket pocket at the same time. And you get ready to tackle him, thinking to yourself, Ah'm bound tae get him this time, he'll never get by me when he's crammin' cake in his mooth, and before you know where you are he's jooked away past you and put in a cross to Owen Mangan or Tommy Duignan and the next thing you know their side's shouting *Goal!* and Fatty McKee is hopping and skipping back up the park, still sookin' his fingers.

I saw Mrs Young up the street the other day, says my mammy.

Oh aye, says my daddy, and how's she keepin'?

Well, you know she's expect . . . You know?

She gives him a look and me a look and then they sit down by the fire and start whispering. It's because they don't want me to hear what they're saying.

It's no use me asking them what they're talking about either.

Ah now never you mind, says my mammy, away and play with your toys. Me and your daddy have something to talk about.

And the two of them start whispering again. They don't even need to whisper because I can't understand a word they're saying anyway, it's all these queer-sounding words I've never heard before, like words they've made up between them. So I kid on I'm playing but in fact I'm watching them like a hawk.

They keep looking round at me all the time.

I'm worried it might be me they're talking about.

But after a while I work it out for myself. They only act like this when they've been talking about some woman we know, like my Auntie Annie or Mrs McNulty from number six. This time it's Mrs Young from Caledonia Street, Auntie Margaret as we call her though she's not really my auntie. So I keep my eyes peeled to see if anything happens and sure enough the next time I see my Auntie Margaret she's swelled up to twice her size. It's the same with any other woman we know. As soon as my mammy and daddy start whispering about her in these wee secret natters of theirs you can bet the next time you see her she'll be swelled up like a balloon.

That's when I start to wonder if they might be doing black magic, casting spells like you read about in the horror comics you get from Yankee Mags up in Wellmeadow. It sounds daft because my mammy and daddy are dead ordinary, in fact to tell the truth I sometimes think they're a bit of a letdown, but that's the way it looks to me with the two of them hunched over the grate whispering the queer words to each other and the fire crackling and spitting behind them. *Black magic*. I don't really believe it, but I don't dare to ask them in case it might be true.

You never know.

Who's your favourite character in history?

Our new class teacher Miss Conlon asks us to think about it for a few minutes then tell the class. We can look at our history book if we like. I like reading about history and writing the compositions though when it comes to the tests I can never remember dates so I don't get high marks.

I kid on I'm thinking but actually I'm looking at Miss

50

Conlon. I love Miss Conlon. I wish I could marry her when I grow up. She's got dark brown wavy hair and a lovely face, like a saint. She always wears nice clothes and she smells like flowers.

When we're saying prayers in the morning Miss Conlon stands at the front of the class with her eyes shut to show us a good example. We're supposed to keep our eyes shut as well, but I spy on her. She looks dead holy with her eyes closed and her long black lashes. But sometimes she opens them to check if McGovern or somebody is acting the goat and she catches me watching her. I kid on I'm just yawning and shut my eyes again.

But I'm still keeking through the slits.

I think I'll say my favourite character is King Richard the Lionheart. I know Miss Conlon likes him as well. He's called that because he was that brave when he led the Christians in the Crusades. The Christians were fighting for Our Lord. The Saracens were fighting for Muhammad. The Christians had straight swords with hilts shaped like the Cross. The Saracens had scimitars with curvy razorsharp blades. They wore flowing robes.

Saracens. Scimitars. Ssss!

Like the swish the blade makes as it slices your head off.

The leader of the Saracens was Saladin.

Saladin was a dashing figure and a strong leader, Miss Conlon tells us, but a sworn enemy of the Christians.

Saladin. I like the name. Too bad he was on their side.

Another favourite of Miss Conlon's that I like is Hereward the Wake. Hereward and his men lived in a secret castle in the Fens that his enemies could never find. The Fens was marshland so you had to be careful where you walked. Marshes are dangerous, like quicksand. One minute you're walking across a grassy field, the next your feet are sinking into the swamp. The more you struggle to get free, the more you get trapped. Nobody can help you because they'd get sucked in too. You sink deeper and deeper and the mud keeps coming up till it fills your mouth and nose and you choke to death. Then you get sucked under the swamp and disappear for ever. The last thing anybody sees is your hand, sticking out above the swamp . . .

The Fens were even worse because there was always mist and fog there so the men hunting Hereward the Wake got lost. They would see lights in the mist and follow them, thinking it was Hereward's men carrying the lights. But no, it was a special kind of light you get in the marsh country called a Jack O'Lantern or a Will o' the Wisp that only leads you deeper and deeper into the swamp. They were doomed.

The Wake is short for the Wakeful, because Hereward was always alert and on the lookout. Hereward and his men knew the marshes inside out. They had a secret pathway across the swamp that looked no different from the ground on either side. The men chasing them could never find the path and perished in the attempt.

My real favourite is Caratacus. He was a chieftain of the ancient Britons who led an uprising against the Roman invader. But they were defeated by the might of Rome and Caratacus got captured. They took Caratacus to Rome and led him through the streets with other prisoners in a victory parade. *But,* says Miss Conlon, reading to us from the history book, *such was the nobility of Caratacus and the dignity of his bearing that the emperor gave him a free pardon.* Her eyes shine when she says this and it makes me sit up straighter in my seat. In the playground I walk around with my head held high and a haughty look. I'm hoping Miss Conlon might look out the staffroom window and see me. *He was just a boy from a poor family,* she'll say one day, *but such was the dignity of his bearing that he stood out from the common herd.*

I'm out the backdoor one night with Wee Alice Cunningham. We've been playing Truth or Dare with Ann Deveney and Rita McNulty but they're away in because it's getting late.

We only stop when Wee Alice has to go to the lavvy in the back of the close.

I wait for her. It's dark now and getting cold, but it's exciting out there in the backdoor, just the two of us. I don't want the game to finish. Neither does she. I can tell.

Lassies pee different fae boays, she says when she comes back.

Och, that's nuthin'. Everyb'dy knows *thaat,* I tell her.

She doesn't say anything back, just stands there looking at me. It's eerie. I can hear the lavvy gurgling in the close.

D'ye want tae see it? she whispers.

Whid'ye mean?

D'ye want me tae show ye?

I can't believe I heard her right.

Whid'ye mean?

It's all I can think of to say.

She's still looking at me.

 53

Cummoan, she says.

She goes into the dark bit at the back of the close and I follow her. I can smell the lavvy smells behind us. The pipes are still hissing.

She slides down the wall and squats on her hunkers. She's footering with her skirt. Something snaps and swishes.

I can't see much. Just her eyes shining up at me.

Cummoan!

I'm a bit feart. Somebody could come out any minute and catch us. But I get down on my hunkers as well.

Ye kin feel it if ye like, she says.

I can hardly breathe. I put out my hand, between her legs. I can feel her knickers, the elastic tight round her ankles, but nothing else. There's nothing there, just a kind of hot breath in my hand.

Tickle it! she says.

She's smiling. I can see her teeth now as well as her eyes.

I put my hand in further, feeling about. Her bare bum, cold and slippy. Then something else, warm and wet. A smell like fish on Friday. My breath sticks in my throat. My trousers are that tight my wullie's sore. My knees are hurting me.

I'm feart. She's Stuart Cunningham's wee sister. If he finds out he'll kill me. If anybody tells my mammy she'll murder me. I don't know what to do.

We hear a voice in the Browns' house.

Whit poaket's it in?

It's Toono's mammy. She's out in the lobby, shouting back in to somebody in the kitchen.

I stand up in a panic.

Ssh! I whisper to Wee Alice. I put my finger to my lips. It smells funny.

54

'S a'right! she whispers.

Ssh! I say again. Then I tiptoe away. I tiptoe all the way up the stairs. My heart's hammering and my head's dizzy. I'm dead feart. I'm listening for Wee Alice to get up and walk out of the close. But I can't hear anything.

She must be still there, in the close.

I wish I was still there with her.

I keep going, up the stairs.

Pat and Mick have been laid off and they're looking for work. And this man tells them about a big contract where they're looking for navvies. The foreman's an Irishman, your man says, so be sure to let him know yiz are from Ireland and yiz'll get fixed up no bother.

But what your man doesn't tell them is that the foreman is Irish all right, but he's an Orangeman from the North.

So Pat and Mick turn up at the site and go lookin' for the foreman. And when they see him, Pat makes the sign of the cross and gives him a big wink and says, Any fear of a job, I don't suppose? And the foreman winks back and kids on he's playing the flute and says, Aye, start on Monday, Ah don't think!

God forgive ye, says my mammy, I don't see what there is to laugh about.

Ah for the love a Mike, says my daddy, can ye no' take a joke?

She doesn't like the Orangemen because they have no time for the Catholics and would never give one a job, not in a month o' Sundays. But the thing she really hates is the Orange Walk. The Orange Walk is a big parade that comes past our street in the summertime. I think it's great because they all wear these bright

Orange sashes and carry big Orange banners on poles and play wee flutes and bang big drums. One thing I don't get is why they have to wear bowler hats and carry rolled-up umbrellas, come rain or come shine. You hardly ever see a man carrying an umbrella in Paisley, it looks sissy. Except for Cuthbert, and he's away in the head.

Did ye ever see anythin' as daftlookin'? says my daddy. Big grownup men carrying them numberellas.

Numberellas. He always says that.

Whit aboot Mister Baird, Daddy? Ye sometimes see him wi' *his* umbrella.

I'm trying to give him a Hint.

Ach it's all right for the likes o' him, says my daddy. A Bigshot like him, he can get away with it. Soft hats, numberellas, all yer orders. Them boys have the money, sure, they can do what they like.

It's true the Orangemen look a bit daft with their wee hats and brollies but it's still a great parade, I always like watching it. But I have to keep quiet about it and make sure I'm out in the street already when it's coming down Underwood Road, so I can walk along beside it with Wullie Deveney or Charlie Miller. Because if I'm still up in the house my mammy will keep me in.

You'll do no such thing, she'll say. Going out mixing with a bunch of oul' bigots and eejits the likes o' them. Bad eggs they are, the lot o' them.

But when the march is going past she always keeks out the slit between the curtains in the big room because that's nearer to Underwood Road and you get a better view. The room's dark because she keeps the heavy curtains shut so the women across the road won't see her. Morton McGrory's mammy and Mrs

Stewart and Mrs Love and the rest of them are all hanging out their windows watching and shouting and laughing back and forth to each other. I don't know why we have to hide in here listening in the dark in the middle of the day. How can she not just push up the window like everybody else and lean out so we can get a better view? But her mouth is tight and she's got this feart, worried look about her so I don't dare to ask.

'The Sash', she whispers to herself, listening. D'ye hear that? They're playing 'The Sash'!

My daddy's telling us one day about this big fella at his work, Big Owney.

He's a Derry man, my daddy says, and begod he hates the Orangemen, he has no time for them at all. And when it comes roun' to the time o' the Orange Walk he goes mad altogether.

Ah but he's great crack all the same, ye have to laugh at him. He lives down there in Caledonia Street somewhere and he was telling us onetime in the hut how he's sick to death o' them Orange . . . soansos marching past his windows. So, says Big Owney, Ah have a gran' idea. Ah'll be stannin' there on the pavement when that big fat drum comes past with that big fat bas— soanso banging away on it. And Ah'll have me big tackety boots on, ready for him. And when they're just going past me Ah'll run out, so Ah will, and Ah'll jump through that effin' drum feet furst!

My daddy's laughing that much when he's telling us this we can hardly make out what he's saying.

My mammy's laughing too, but she's shaking her head.

Ah God help him, she says. I hope ye think it. Sure

they'd batter the poor fella half to death, the same Orangemen.

Sure we told him that! says my daddy. And d'ye know what he said? Begod, siz he, won't it be worth it? Every punch and kick of it. And when Ah get dragged up in front of the court after for disturbing the peace, Ah have me story all ready for the judge.

What're ye gonna tell him Owney? O' coorse we're all eggin' him on, like, ye know, playin' up to him. And d'ye know what he says?

Well lads, siz Owney, When the oul' sourpuss of a judge asks me, Do you have anything to say in your defence? Ah'll tell him, Yes surr, yir honour, I do indeed.

Oh? he'll say. And what might that be?

Yir Honour, Ah'll say to him – and Ah'll have the oul' chest stuck out and the head high. Yir honour, Ah have filled a lifetime ambition!

My daddy's got it wrong. He means *ful*filled.

But it doesn't matter, it's still dead funny.

He's wiping the tears from his eyes with the back of his hand.

Ah jaisus, he says, that's Big Owney for ye. He'd make ye die laughin'.

He sits up dead straight and serious, imitating Big Owney.

Yir honour, siz he, Ah have filled a lifetime ambition!

Korky the Cat is on the cover of the *Dandy* and in the *Beano* it's Biffo the Bear in his wee short trousers with the bib and braces. Desperate Dan's got a big stubbly chin and he always wears this daft wee Stetson and his six-shooter and he likes to eat big cow pies with the horns sticking out. Lord Snooty's real name is Marmaduke and he lives in a fancy castle with his pals and they're always getting up to no good and coming to a sticky end, though the next week they're back again, good as new, and up to their old shenanigans. Jimmy and his Magic Patch is a boy with a bit of magic carpet on the seat of his trousers and whenever he touches it he's whisked away through time to adventures in foreign lands.

The *Dandy* comes out on Tuesday and the *Beano*'s on Thursday. They're my favourite comics but I can hardly ever buy them because I don't get pocket money, so I have to try and get the lend of them off somebody that does. Charlie Miller gets pocket money and most days the two of us walk back to Galloway Street from school, so on *Dandy* and *Beano* days I'm hoping he'll buy it on the way home. Of course I always know when it's *Dandy* or *Beano* day, but Charlie sometimes forgets. He's not very clever, in fact to tell you the truth he's a bit slow, he's in the dunces' row in our class. But he's dead touchy as well so you have to watch it. I can't just suddenly come out with Hey Charlie, it's Tuesday, ye gonnae buy the *Dandy*? because that would give the game away altogether. He might go in a huff and not buy it at all, or if he does he might not let me read it and what good would that be?

We walk along past Love Street where my daddy sometimes takes me to watch St Mirren, even though we're Celtic supporters. There's a wee row of shops just after the high wall outside St Mirren's ground, and that's where the newsagent's is, so I have to start dropping hints to Charlie before we get there. Of course I do it in a roundabout way so Charlie'll think it was his idea.

Ah wish it wis Friday, eh Charlie?

That's safe enough, we're always wishing it was Friday.

Whit? Oh, aye!

Only Wensday the day, intit?

Of course I know fine what day it is but I can't just come straight out and say it.

Is it? Ye sure? Ah thoat it wis . . . Is it no' Tuesday the day?

Jings, Charlie, ye're right. So it is. It's Tuesday, right enough.

Now I keep quiet for a while hoping the penny will drop in Charlie's head and maybe the tuppence will come out of his pocket. But nothing doing. Charlie's started aiming spits at old cigarette packets in the gutter.

I better get his mind off that quick, before he turns it into a game.

Hey, wait a minute, Charlie!

Whit?

Tuesday! Thur's sumthin Ah wis tryin' tae remember aboot Tuesday . . .

Whit is it?

Och Ah don't know. Ah forget . . . Can *you* no' think a sumthin? Sumthin aboot Tuesday?

Naw. Eh . . . It's a long time tae Friday?

Aye Charlie, so it is . . . but that's no whit Ah wis thinkin' aboot. Tuesday . . . Tuesday . . . Whit wis it?

I start chapping my forehead kidding on I'm trying to think. We don't say anything for a while and I'm getting desperate. We're past the shops already and coming up to the gates of the Fountain Gardens and once we're in there it'll be too late.

Hey wait a minnit, Charlie says.

Whit? Whit is it?

Tuesday! Is it no' the day the *Dandy* comes oot?

Whit? Oh aye, so it is, Charlie, ye're right enough. That's no what Ah wis thinkin' aboot, mind . . .

I'm still trying to act casual but I don't need to bother because Charlie's turned round and away back to the newsagent's to get the *Dandy*.

The next bit is much harder. We're dawdling through the Fountain Gardens because Charlie's reading his *Dandy*. He'll let me look at it over his shoulder, he says, but I always say No because I've got other plans.

Naw, Charlie, I say, dead noble. It's your comic, you read it. Ah'll jist have a wee read when you're finished.

I'm taking a big risk here. Charlie's terrible at reading, he's one of the slowest in the class. But I'm trying to put the idea in his head that I'm waiting, I'm next after him, hoping he'll hurry up. Charlie's dead good natured and he's my pal; he'll not like to think he's keeping me waiting. It's one of the reasons I like him.

Still, I have to wait till he finishes the first page before I can make my next move.

It takes for ever. Charlie keeps staring at the pictures and the wee balloons with the words in them and I can hear him half whispering the words to himself the way my daddy does when he's reading the *Daily Record*, except with Charlie's asthma the whispers come out all wheezy. Sometimes I catch him looking back at bits he's already read and wheezing away under his breath and it nearly drives me mad. I feel like ripping the comic out of his hand. But of course I don't because Charlie would probably thump me and that would be the end of that.

61

We're nearly through the Fountain Gardens and into Caledonia Street before Charlie turns the page. I look at him as if I'm amazed.

Jings, Charlie, d'ye mean tae say ye've finished that page already?

I'm taking an even bigger risk now, because Charlie's not that stupid, not really, he *knows* he's a slow reader. If he thinks for a minute I'm taking the mickey he'll mollecate me, so I have to keep talking.

Ah mean, Ah know Miss Conlon's always saying ye're slow 'n that, but when ye're readin' sumthin ye *like*, ye're dead fast, so ye are!

It works. Charlie hardly ever gets compliments at school and especially not for his reading so this goes to his head altogether and he starts zipping through the rest of the comic like the Wells Fargo express. And every time he turns the page I let out this wee *Phwoof!* kidding on I'm amazed how fast he can read.

We're just through the wee tunnel under the railway at the bottom end of Underwood Road when Charlie hands over the comic, so I could easily read half of it before we get to Galloway Street. But of course I'm in no hurry now, I take my time, I just keep telling Charlie that I'm not as fast a reader as him. So when we get to my close at number four I'm only half-way through Desperate Dan.

I look up, a bit sad, and hand the comic back to Charlie.

Och, naw, he says. Ye kin hing oantae it fur a while. Jist tae ye've finished it, OK?

Sometimes Charlie's that innocent it makes me ashamed. It makes me think about what old Miss O'Neill used to tell us about our Conscience.

Think of it as the voice of your Guardian Angel. It's

*that wee quiet voice that whispers inside your head,
telling you what's right and what's wrong. And of
course we should always listen to our Guardian Angel,
shouldn't we?*

But my Guardian Angel could be screaming in my
ear for all the good it does.

Aw thanks, Charlie, I say. Ah'll gie it back tae ye the
morra.

When I'm saying this I always mean it at the time.
But the truth is I've got a wee collection of *Dandy*s and
*Beano*s planked under the bed and I got them all off
Charlie.

1949

Big Owen Mangan and Tommy Duignan pick the teams
for football in the playground. They're the captains,
the best players. The rest of us stand in a line and hope
they'll call out our names.

Fatty!

That's Fatty McKee. He always gets picked first.

Flash!

Flash Anderson. He's a great runner.

Foley!

It must be great when they call out your name early:
you walk out there and stand beside your captain, dead
proud.

You've been picked. He wants you on his side.

McColl!

McKean!

It's all right for the good players; all they have to
worry about is whose side they'll be on. But I'm always
feart: *what if I'm last?*

63

Kiernan!

Miller!

The names keep getting called out and the line's getting shorter and still nobody's picked me. Me and the other boys stand there trying to look as if we don't care.

I'm sick in my heart: *how come they don't pick me?*

I know why. I'm quite big and solid and not bad with my right foot but I get dead nervous when the ball comes to me. I'm feart I'll make a mess of it so I get rid of it as soon as I can, boot it up the park, anywhere. Big Owen gets fed up with me when I'm playing on his side.

Haud oantae it, Boyle, he says. Watch whit yer daein'! Keep the heid!

I know he's right but I just can't do it. I get feart I'll do something daft and put myself to shame. The good players are not like that: they *want* the ball; they shout for it, they charge in and tackle for it. Then they run with it, dribbling and jinking and doing fancy stuff like Fatty McKee. Big Owen never panics, even when he's surrounded by players from the other side. He takes his time, looks round. He never just gets rid of the ball; he passes it, crosses, shoots.

How does he do it?

Big Owen'll never pick me again. The last time we played, the ball came to me right in front of the goals. A sitter. All I had to do was shoot. I couldn't do it, feart I'd miss. I passed it back to Fatty, thinking, He's a good player, he deserves it, he's bound to score. But Fatty was surrounded, he got tackled and lost the ball.

Chricesake, Boyle! he said. How d'ye no' jist shoot?

Big Owen didn't shout at me. It was worse: he didn't say anything, just looked at me, shaking his head.

Hopeless.

McClardie!

McGovern!

There's only three of us left: me, Michael Daley and Wee Joe Moore; it means we're the duffers. We look at each other; it's easier than facing the ones who've been picked. We shrug, try to laugh, kid on we're not bothered. But I'm praying, *Please God, don't let me be last.*

Boyle!

It's Big Owen. Thank God for that. I walk out, trying to act casual. But he's saved my life. I'll try my hardest for him. He'll never be sorry he picked me.

Duignan calls out Daley's name and now there's only one boy left standing there. Wee Joe Moore. He's not that wee, not really, just dead skinny. He's dead scruffy as well and a good fighter and to tell the truth I'm a bit feart of him, but he's hopeless at football and that's why he's last. Odd man out, no room at the inn. He'll still get a game; he'll just get tacked onto one of the teams. They'll be a man extra but nobody will argue.

Who cares? He's hopeless anyway, last to get picked.

I feel a bit sorry for Wee Joe Moore, but not too much. I'm just glad it's not me.

One day Miss Conlon tells the class about a great idea she's had.

It's called Penfriends, she says. You all write letters to boys and girls in a school in another country and they write back to you. It'll help you with your hand-writing and your composition and you'll learn something about how people live in that country, and who knows? You might even become friends for life. God works in mysterious ways, Miss Conlon says.

She's talked to Mother Stanislaus and they've already picked out a school in Nigeria in Africa that's run by the White Fathers. I'm a wee bit disappointed, to tell you the truth, I'd have preferred the Wild West of America or Australia's sunny shore, but still . . .

All the boys have to write letters to boys of our own age in Nigeria and the lassies have to do the same. We don't know the names of our penfriends yet: we won't know that till they reply.

I write about Galloway Street, how we live at the top of a tenement four storeys high and how I've got a sister and two wee brothers now, though wee Vincent's just a baby. I write about playing football in the street, and bools and peeries. I say I support Celtic and especially Charlie Tully and do they play football in Nigeria? And I tell him about Miss Conlon and St James's.

After I've posted the letter I think maybe I should have mentioned the black babies, because he might have been one, with him going to school with the White Fathers and that. I wonder if it could even be my own black baby, wee Richard. You never know, God works in mysterious ways.

It's great when the replies start arriving with the foreign stamps. Our Nigerian penfriends have all got funny names like Aloysius Nkobe and Stanislaus Mogawatu. That's quite normal, Miss Conlon tells us: children at the missionary schools get Christian names when they're baptized, but their family names are still African.

When my letter comes my penfriend's name is not Richard after all, it's Archibald.

Archibald Mtombe, I tell my pal Toono down in the close.

66

Archie McToambey, eh? says Toono. That's a guid Scoattish name.

That's the trouble with Toono, he's a bit of a smart alec.

So I don't tell him the other thing about the letter, the bit about Archie asking me for money.

I like your letter very much [Archie writes]. I think you and your family have a good life there in Great Britain. Unfortunately me and my four brothers and three sisters are poor. My father works hard every day to feed us. Unfortunately it is not enough for a large family. I am big and strong, I need plenty to eat. So please will you send us some money to buy food? It will be very kind of you, I am sure you can spare it . . .

It goes on like that for three pages and in the end I show it to my mammy because I don't know what to do.

In the name o' God, she says, what were ye saying in yer letter to make him think we're well off? Jesus Mary and Joseph, do they think we're living the life o' Riley here, or what? *Send them some money indeed* – and me with barely enough to feed ye all and put clothes on your backs!

I'm to show the letter to Miss Conlon, she says, because somebody will have to put a stop to this carry-on.

Miss Conlon shows the letter to Mother Stanislaus and the two of them stand there for a while frowning and whispering, then Miss Conlon says it's all right for me to write back but not to say anything about the money.

Mother Stanislaus will write to the White Fathers,

she says, and they'll have a word with Archibald, don't worry.

So I write him another letter about Celtic beating Raith Rovers 3–0 last week and about my favourite stories in the *Dandy* and the *Beano*. And I tell him about Oor Wullie and The Broons in the *Sunday Post.*

When Archie writes back it's just one page with very neat handwriting in pen and ink on both sides, and it's all about how nice their school is in Nigeria and how kind the White Fathers are and how they're hoping to get a new pump for their village with the help of God. And it's signed at the bottom, Yours sincerely, Your Nigerian Penfriend, Archibald Mtombe. But there's a wee note in beside it scribbled in pencil:

Please, when you send the money do not mention it to Missis Conlon, it must be a secret between us. Your Friend, Archibald.

And though I feel like a traitor, my mammy makes me show this to Miss Conlon. The next thing is, Tommy Duignan and Danny McKean start getting letters from their penfriends asking for money as well. We're wondering whether they came up with this off their own bat, or if it's just pals of Archie's copying his idea, but we never find out because that's the last we hear from Miss Conlon about our Nigerian penfriends.

Frankie's dead embarrassing when we're out in the street. He thinks because I talk to him in bed at night we should be pals during the day as well. He can never get it into his head that wee brothers belong to a different world. Now he's got a wee brother of his own, wee Vincent the new baby, you'd think he'd get the message. But no. He always wants to be in the same team as me at football when they're picking sides, and that's embarrassing enough, but it's worse when I want to go places with Toono and the gang and he tries to follow me.

Our gang is me, Wullie Deveney, Charlie Miller and Toono. And sometimes Flash Anderson though he lives down the other end of Galloway Street and we don't see him much. Toono's the best fighter so he's the leader of the gang, even though he's the only Proddy. He goes about with us because he lives in the same close as me and Wullie. He doesn't get on with Morton McGrory or Stuart Cunningham from across the street even though they're Protestants as well.

Toono's his nickname. His real name is Alan Brown and he got into a fight with Morton McGrory one day because McGrory was trying to take the mickey, chanting,

> *Alan Broon*
> *Went up the toon*
> *An' fell in a pile*
> *O' toleys.*

They had a fight and Toono duffed McGrory up. That's when it started, the nickname. Toono must like being called that because you'd soon know if he didn't. He'd hit you.

Sometimes we go searching for the Lucky Middens. They're bins round the backdoors of posh houses where the Toffs live and sometimes you get gold and silver things mixed in with their rubbish. Toono's the only one who knows where they are.

Ye can strike it rich at the Lucky Middens, he says.

He takes us up to the posh houses at Castlehead and we rummage through the bins for old kettles and teapots and broken china. If it's metal Toono rubs it and squints at it dead serious through this old lens he got off a pair of broken specs, like a jeweller in the pictures. That's silver, he says, and in the sack it goes. He does the same with the broken china. That's pore-salane, he says. Sometimes we find old bangles or necklaces or brooches. There's nearly always a bangle that's pure gold and a necklace of precious diamonds. Aye, says Toono, that's the real McCoy, a' right, and in the sack they go. Then we run away home to divvy up the treasure. Toono's Ali Baba so he gets to keep the best stuff. Me and Wullie and Charlie are only the Forty Thieves so we get the rest.

The funny thing is, it always feels like real treasure when we're hiding round the back of the posh house and whispering and putting the stuff in the sack, but when we're back in the backdoors in Galloway Street it just looks like old junk, a dented kettle with no lid and an old teapot with its spout all squeegeee and a few glass beads on an old bit of string. At least that's what I think though naturally I never say anything. But it makes no difference, because anytime Ali Baba feels like going on a raid of the Lucky Middens the Forty Thieves are always ready and willing to back him up.

But first we have to get rid of Frankie because he'll follow us. It's no use me saying he can't come, he'll just start greetin'.

Ah'm gonnae tell oan you, he'll say.

He knows my mammy doesn't like me going places with Toono because she thinks he'll get me into trouble.

I have no time for that Toono, she says. A toerag and an ignoramus, that's all he is.

She doesn't like him because he's a Proddy.

We work out a wee trick to get rid of Frankie. We kid on we're all going home. Charlie says he's going back to number eight and me and Frankie and Wullie and Toono go in the close at number four. Then Toono says he's got to go to the lavvy out the back first and Wullie says so does he and he'll go next. So me and Frankie start going up the stairs. When we get to the second landing Toono shouts up to us.

Hey Johnny! Come back doon a minute. There's something I forgot to tell you. A secret.

He means me. Johnny's my gang name.

Jist go up the hoose, I tell Frankie. I'll be coming up in a minute.

But he won't go. He's suspicious. He just stands there.

Awright then, just wait on the landing for me. OK?

I run back down the stairs. Toono and Wullie are waiting with Charlie Miller at the front of our close and we run like mad to get away before Frankie sees us. But Wullie and Charlie start giggling and snorting before we even get out of the close so he's bound to hear us.

We're in Brown's Place and nearly at the swings when we hear him. He's greetin' and shouting at the same time.

You're rotten, so ye are. Ah'm tellin' ma mammy on you, John Boyle!

He's standing in front of our close making that much racket the whole street can hear him. I'm feart our window is going to go flying up any minute. We jook in behind the houses near the swings. We can still hear Frankie roarin' and greetin' and I feel rotten because he's my wee brother but I'm raging mad as well. He's embarrassing me. The other boys in the gang are killing themselves laughing. It's all right for them.

Wait tae Ah get that wee soanso, I tell them. Ah'll murder 'um, so Ah will.

I say it dead serious, so they'll know I'm in earnest.

Sometimes when I'm up the street I see Cuthbert.

You'd never think it to look at him, but Cuthbert's not right in the head. He's always well dressed in a light gabardine coat with polished brown brogues and a black brolly hooked over his arm. If a man carries a brolly in Paisley they call him a sissy, but you'd have to have a screw loose yourself to call Cuthbert a sissy because people are a bit feart of him. The scary thing about Cuthbert is, he looks quite normal and respectable till you get near him then you notice he's talking to himself. He blethers away quite the thing and smiles and nods as if there's somebody else walking along beside him. And in Cuthbert's mind, there probably is.

Whenever I see Cuthbert coming I cross over to the other side of the road and pray to God he'll not notice me. One time I'm up near Well Street with Toono and Toono shouts across to him, Ye a' right there Cuthbert? And Cuthbert gives us a big smile and waves his brolly and shouts back, All right! All right!

It's a sin, intit? Toono says through his teeth when he's smiling back. *The man's a loony. The heid's away.*

I don't like it when Toono does this because it's dead sleekit and I feel sorry for Cuthbert. And I'm feart what would happen if Cuthbert heard him. People say he's harmless, but I'm not so sure. Sometimes he'll get excited for no reason that you can see and start running along the pavement roaring and whirling his brolly round like the big hand on the clock when you're winding it up. Then he'll slow down and walk and start blethering again. He's not that tall but stocky, with a broad, bony head and short springy hair. I think if he came at you he'd be like a charging bull; you'd need a sledgehammer or something to stop him.

Ah it's a shame about him, says my mammy when I ask her, God help him, the craitchur. And him from a very welltodo family, too. His father was a Bigshot up there in Castlehead or Thornly Park, a doctor or something, with letters after his name anyway. And Cuthbert was a medical student, or so they say, going to be a doctor himself. And he was too clever altogether and must have studied too hard or something and it did something to his brain. There ye are now, *ahashki*, let that be a lesson to ye. Amn't I always telling ye? Too much thinking and reading and dreaming and doting can be bad for ye. God save the mark, ye might end up like Cuthbert if ye're not careful.

Something bad's happened.

It's the day of the Orange Walk. I've been out playing in the backdoors with Wullie and Charlie and I'm coming in because it's dark. As soon as I walk in I hear somebody bawling and greetin' in the big room.

My mammy's standing by the sink, listening. Her face and mouth are tight. She hardly looks at me.

It's Margaret I can hear in the room. My daddy's in there with her with the door shut and he's giving her the belt.

Margaret never gets the belt. Me and Frankie get it when we do something really bad and my mammy tells my daddy on us, but he never hits Margaret because she's a lassie.

73

He's hitting her now. I can hear the whacks and the screams coming through the door.

My mammy won't tell me what's wrong.

Never you mind, she says. She has to learn to do what she's told and that's all about it. It'll teach her a lesson. Brought up to the door by the polis, giving us the fright of our lives. It's ashamed she should be.

The door opens and my daddy comes out.

That'll learn ye, he says, over his shoulder.

He shuts it behind him.

I can still hear her whimpering and sniffing in the room.

I'm feart.

Whit is it Daddy?

Never you mind, he says.

He doesn't even look at me. He walks past me with his eyes flickering down and to the side and hangs the big belt back up on its nail in the lobby.

His face looks funny. You'd think he'd been greetin'.

Somebody's at the door and my mammy goes to see who it is because my hair's all wet; she's been washing it in the basin in front of the fire and going through it with the finetooth comb, looking for nits. I hear her opening the door, then nothing. I don't hear her shutting it again. I wonder why she's just standing out there with the door open.

What is it, son? I hear her saying after a while. What's the matter?

I can hear somebody whispering on the landing. It sounds like Charlie. Then my mammy again.

No, son, John can't come out now, he's getting his hair washed.

More mumbling, then she calls in to me.

John? Come out here a minute will ye?

I don't like the sound of her voice. I'm a bit embarrassed to go out there with my vest all wet and my head wrapped in the towel like an Arab, but I have to go.

Sure enough it's Charlie, and the reason he took so long to talk is because his asthma is very bad and he's all puffed out and wheezy after climbing up our stairs.

Have you been getting the lend of Charlie's comics and not giving them back? says my mammy. She's not too pleased by the sound of it.

Charlie looks dead embarrassed.

Ah'm sorry, John, he says in his wheezy voice. Ma mammy sent me tae get them back.

He means the *Dandy*s and *Beano*s I've been collecting under the bed in the big room. I was hoping he forgot all about them. Some hope.

Oh, right. Ye mean last week's *Dandy* and *Beano*?

I'm trying to sound casual, as if to say: Ah wis gonnae gi'e ye them back, whit's yer hurry?

Charlie looks that miserable I feel sorry for him.

Eh well . . . Naw. She says Ah've tae get them *aw* back.

My mammy gives me a hard look. She knows.

She makes me get under the bed and pull out the stoury pile of comics. There must be about twenty of them, easy.

Give the boy back his comics, she says. That's terrible, so it is. It's ashamed ye should be.

She sends me back out to hand the whole pile over to Charlie on the landing.

Ah'm sorry, John, he wheezes at me. Ah couldnae help it, honest. It wis ma mammy.

And away he goes back down the stairs with his

*Dandy*s and *Beano*s. He's nearly greetin'. I feel a bit sorry for him.

I feel even sorrier when we're back sitting by the fire with the finetooth comb and my mammy keeps digging it into my head. She won't even show me the nit any more before she cracks it with her fingernail and throws it in the fire. She just drags the comb hard across my head and tuts when I complain.

Arra don't be such a big baby, she says. Grow up.

I just have to take it. It's my penance for Charlie's comics.

Poor Pat's been seen in Coventry, down in England. A woman from Achill that Mrs Young knows was passing through and swears it was him she saw driving past in a Corporation bus.

Ah Poor Pat, says my mammy, God help him. I hope it was him. That's a good steady job, a bus driver.

I'm glad for her, but it's a bit of a letdown all the same. I liked it better when he was on the ships.

I get Margaret on her own on the landing and ask her what happened the day of the Orange Walk.

Ah followed the band, she says. An' Ah got lost.

I can hardly believe it. I'd never dare to follow the Orange Walk. Sometimes me and Wullie and Charlie follow them down Underwood Road as far as the railway arch, but we'd never go any further than that. I don't even know where they go after that.

The racecourse, she says. They go tae the racecourse.

The racecourse! That's miles away! How d'ye know they go there?

Ah told ye, Ah followed them.

I make her tell me the whole story.

She's out playing beds in Galloway Street, she says, when she hears music and drums coming down Underwood Road. A parade. People are running up to the corner to watch so she goes as well.

There's that many people she can't get through so the only way she can see is to stand up on Galbraith's windowsill and grab on with her fingers to the steel shutters.

She sees big square banners in bright colours flapping on high poles and men wearing bright orange sashes and bowler hats. There's men playing flutes and drums and one man beating a gigantic round drum he keeps balanced on his belly.

BOOM!

BOOM!

BOOM!

BOOM!

With the flutes playing and the drums pounding and the flags and banners waving it's the most exciting thing she's ever seen. She stands there at Galbraith's window hanging on with one hand and waving with the other and she hopes it'll never stop.

So when the band goes away past she has to follow. The crowd on the pavement starts breaking up so she can squeeze through into the road behind the parade. There's other weans there, though none she knows, all skipping along like her and clapping their hands to the music.

BOOM!

BOOM!

BOOM!

BOOM!

She tells me how she follows the music all the way past the railway arch and round the corner into

Caledonia Street. How exciting it is to be skipping along in the middle of the road, not bothered about motors or buses, with the crowds waving at her and cheering her on both sides. After a while some of the other weans leave the procession, but new ones join in, skipping and laughing.

I try to picture Margaret among these weans following the music, like the weans that followed the Pied Piper of Hamelin, and I feel I hardly know my wee sister.

I feel sorry for her. And feart as well.

Along Caledonia Street something funny starts to happen. The people on the pavement are still cheering but other people behind them are effing and blinding. Most of the women hanging out their windows are smiling and waving but there are other ones that are angry and shouting curses.

An' then, Margaret says, Ah see these big green clods comin' flyin' over people's heads and smashin' intae the parade.

When she tells me this I can't help smiling. I can't help thinking about Big Owney waiting on the pavement in his tackety boots. Caledonia Street is near where he lives and I can just picture him and his pals digging up the clods out the backdoors and stacking them up for ammunition.

Men in the parade start shouting and swearing back. Every so often there's a big row and the parade has to slow down while the polis come in and calm things down. One time the whole parade comes to a dead stop, but the marchers just keep marching on the spot, the band keeps playing the flutes and banging the drums and the weans at the back keep on skipping and dancing.

Wur ye no' feart? I ask her.

Ah thought it wis jist part o' the parade, she says. Like at the Shows or Sports Day at school.

For God's sake, how innocent kin ye get? I scoff at her. It wis the Orange Walk!

Her face crumples.

Ah didnae know, she says. How wis Ah tae know?

I can see she's thinking back to when she was getting the belt from my daddy. She'll start greetin' any minute.

Och, it's a'right! I tell her. It wisnae your fault. How were ye tae know? Jist tell me whit happened.

She tells me how the march moved on. How the flutes started playing a different tune, a great tune, she says, and the marchers were singing along in time to the music.

D'ye remember whit tune it wis? I ask her.

DEE-da-DEE-da-DEE-da-DEE da-da, she chants, slapping out the rhythm with her hand on her knee.

Shhh, for God's sake, I hiss at her, looking around us. Sumdy might hear ye.

It's 'The Sash' she's chanting. I know the tune. I even know some of the words.

> Oh my father was an Orangeman
> In the days of long ago . . .

They were singing it at the tops of their voices, Margaret says. They were singing it to the people standing on the pavement, the women at the windows, the men behind the crowds shouting and cursing and slinging the clods. Between the flutes and the drums and the singing and shouting and the tramping feet, it was more noise than Margaret had ever heard. And she

79

was right in the middle of it. She'd never seen anything as exciting in her life.

> *An' we'll hing the Pope!*
> *Wi' a taury rope!*
> *An' the sash my father wore!*

And on they marched, to the end of Caledonia Street then along the Greenock Road, past the priest's house where Father Murphy lives and on past the place where they're building the new St James's Church. They marched and whistled and drummed all the way along that long road and into the racecourse.

Ah told ye, says Margaret. Where we go tae the Shows. An' they had all these buses and vans there, just like the Shows.

Oh aye, I say, Ah see whit ye mean.

What's the use of arguing with her? Anyway I want to hear the rest.

But as it turns out, not much else happened. When they got to the racecourse the band stopped playing and they all gathered round in a big crowd listening to men standing on the back of a van making speeches.

Like when the priest says the sermon at Mass, she says.

Aye, that'll be right.

That's what I'm thinking, but I don't say it.

She didn't understand what the men were saying and she didn't care. All she knew was there were no merrygorounds or bumpercars at these Shows, no wee stalls where you can win dolls or balloons. And no sign of the band anywhere. The weans who'd been with her on the parade had all disappeared. She was getting fed up now, and worried. All she could think

80

about was when the music would start up again, so she could follow the band back home.

When the last man finished speaking there was a huge roar and the crowd cheered and clapped for a long time. Then all of a sudden everybody was in a hurry. People were shouting and waving to each other and rushing past her this way and that pushing and shoving to get on the buses. She stood there watching as one by one the buses started up and pulled away. The singing started up again on some of them but it wasn't the same. Still no sign of the band. She stood there watching as the last bus drove away down the road and there was no music now, no drums or flutes, nothing left around her but the empty racecourse and the darkening sky.

My mammy is always sending me out to get messages. Usually it's just up to Galbraith's at the corner for a sliced pan loaf or round to Jimmy Canning's general store for totties or turnips or a packet of washing powder. I always want to get Persil because Persil Washes Whiter, it says on the posters, And It Shows. But we get Rinso because it's better value, my mammy says. And five Woodbine for my daddy because they're the cheapest cigarettes, though he's always complaining afterwards.

Arra what use is five fags to a workin' man? Could ye no' get me ten for wance, like everybody else?

But it's always five because he smokes too much anyway, she says, and it's bad for him. Sometimes he gets a packet of ten with money he's kept back but then he puts them in this steel cigarette case he found on the bus one time and he throws the packet away because he knows if she sees it she'll only ask him where he got the money to buy ten Woodbine.

By God you must think it's well off we are, she'll say. Throwing money away on cigarettes to go puffing up in smoke.

My daddy quite likes Woodbine, though he always acts embarrassed when he offers one to a visitor, especially if it's Mr Baird the insurance man when he's standing blethering to my mammy in the kitchen.

It'd shame ye, my daddy says afterwards, Offering Woodbine to a Bigshot like that.

Arra isn't it good enough for him? my mammy says. It's glad of it he should be. He's too sweet to be wholesome, the same Mr Baird, always blethering out of him. I'm not too sure about him, Bigshot or no Bigshot.

The insurance man is a Bigshot because he wears a soft hat. My daddy wears a bunnet.

It's oney Woodbine, I'm afraid, he says when he holds out the packet to Mr Baird. He gives it a wee shake so the cigarettes stick out a bit.

But Woodbine or no Woodbine they smoke them anyway and sometimes he gets a Capstan or a Player's back when it's the insurance man's turn, so he's dead pleased.

Player's, eh? he says to me afterwards. That's a grand cigarette! Begod I did well there.

He hardly ever gets Capstan or Player's.

Yer mammy would go mad altogether, he tells me, and he jerks his head back and his eyes roll up so you can only see the white bits. Then he tuts and sighs this hopeless way he does sometimes, you'd think it was the end of the world.

Capstan Full Strength. Player's Please. Player's has a great picture on the packet: a man with a nice face and a big dark beard and a peaked sailor cap, framed in a lifebelt with rope twined round it. Is this what my Uncle Pat looks like?

I don't mind going to Jimmy Canning's because it's just round the corner. Jimmy Canning is a quiet man with a bunnet and a thin yellowy face and glasses. When he's adding up you can hear him breathing through his nose because he's nearly always got a cigarette stuck in his mouth with a long grey ash on it.

There's always smells in the shop because he's got sacks of stuff like lentils and split peas and barley open on the floor, and packets of tea and sugar and flour on the shelves. He gets the lentils out of the sack with a metal scoop he has and pours them into a brown paper poke that he stands on the scales. I like the swoosh the lentils make when they're pouring into the poke. He puts wee brass weights on the other side of the scale then he'll take some lentils back out with the scoop or shake more in till the two scales balance and that's the right amount. There are big sweetie jars up on the shelves behind the counter. Dolly Mixtures. Bullseyes. Caramels. Fox's Glacier Mints. He keeps penny caramels and gobstoppers and lollipops on the counter beside the big tin of broken biscuits because they're what the weans usually come in to buy.

But not us. Well, hardly ever.

We have no coupons in the ration book for the likes of that oul' rubbish, my mammy says when we ask her.

But I know she swaps our sweetie coupons. She knows a Mrs Corrigan who's a cousin or something from Ireland that keeps a chip shop up at the West End. This woman takes the sweetie coupons off her and gives her something else back, food coupons or money, I don't remember. I know about it because I was with her one time she went there and I heard them talking.

They're not supposed to do that, it's not fair. But I don't say anything. It would only put her in a bad mood.

Sometimes I have to go farther away, up to the Co-operative Stores near the gasworks for a big tin of National Dried Milk or a jar of Extract of Malt. The Co-operative is her favourite shop, she says, because you get the Divvy. And once in a while she sends me all the way to the shops up at Well Street usually for butcher meat, half a pound of mince or liver or half a pound of slice, even though she knows we all like links better.

Slice is better value for money, she says. Them links are too dear altogether.

Sure aren't they all the bliddy same? my daddy complains. Isn't it the same sausages, oney different shapes?

Oney. He always says that. He means only.

We only get links when he's the one that gets the butcher meat on his way home from work. But it's always slice she puts down when she writes out her wee list on a bit of paper and folds it tight inside the ration book with a ten shilling note or a pound.

Be sure and bring home the right change now, she says to me, and don't dillydally either, dreaming and doting about the place the way you do half the time.

She says that because she sent me up to Well Street for butcher meat one time in the winter and I must have dillydallied because by the time I got there it was getting dark and the shop lights were all on. It was foggy as well and everything looked different from the daytime and I got lost. I asked this woman where the butcher's was. Let me look in your ration book, son, she said, to see what it is your mammy wants. Then

84

she showed me where the shop was. It was in the same place it always was except it felt different at night but when it was time to pay for the messages there was no pound note in the ration book.

Would you believe that? my mammy says when she tells people. And her that well dressed and well spoken, too. The Lord bless us and save us, tonight and tomorra, who would believe a woman could do such a thing to a child?

My daddy comes in from his work and has his wash at the sink then sits down to his totties. Whatever he's getting for his dinner, there's always plenty of totties.

He likes Golden Wonders best, piled up on his plate steaming hot with their skins still on. The skin on the old totties is dark and thick, on the new ones it's pale and skimpy. He spears a totty on his fork and peels the skin off with his knife or uses his thick fingers.

The fingertips and nails on his right hand are a darker colour, yellowy brown. That's what he gets for smoking, my mammy says.

The signs'll be by ye, she says. Ye'll come to a bad end.

His brown fingers make the peeled totty look all creamy and white.

When he's in a good mood and not too tired he'll peel a totty for me, even though I've had my dinner. Then he hands it to me on the fork.

Houl' on to that now, youngfella, he says, till Ah put a bit o' salt on it. Totties is not the same without a good pinch o' salt.

He puts a wee daud of butter in a saucer for me and rolls the peeled totty in it, still stuck on the fork. Then he sprinkles salt on it and a bit of pepper and hands it back to me.

I know what to do next because I've watched him doing it millions of times.

I hold the fork and blow on the totty to cool it. Then I test it with the edge of my teeth, the way you do with an ice lolly, just a nibble at first.

I have to keep blowing till it cools down.

He watches me taking my first bite and laughs because it's that burny I have to roll it about my mouth with my tongue and sook air in through my teeth before I can eat it.

It tastes delicious though.

There now, he says. What d'ye think o' that, eh? Isn't that lovely? Ah ye can't beat the good oul shpud. It's the salt o' the earth.

He gets stuck in to the mountain on his plate.

Saturday afternoons are great because we go to the matinée at the Bug Hut and see Buster Crabbe and Charlie Chaplin and Laurel and Hardy. Its real name is the Astoria Picture House in Lawn Street, but everybody calls it the Bug Hut because it's a dump and they say it's hoachin' with fleas. The bit where you go in off the street and pay your ninepence looks all right, but then you have to stand in a freezing passage with open sides that let the wind and rain in and a corrugated iron roof that leaks and you're all bunched up in a queue because the checkie's standing up the front with a big rope stretched across so nobody can get by. There's always a terrible echoey racket in the passage especially with the rain battering down on the iron roof and the weans all shouting at the same time. The old pensioners that come in for the cheap prices are stuck in the middle of all this pandemonium and you'd feel sorry for them except they're always moaning about the noise. The checkie's supposed to keep us quiet but he ends up shouting louder than everybody else.

Right, he shouts. That's enough! Keep that noaise doon or yeez'll get chucked oot! Ah'm warning yeez!

And for a while it works: everything goes quiet and we all start whispering because we're feart we might get flung out right enough, though at the same time we're trying not to laugh because the idea of getting barred from the Astoria is dead funny. The Boy that got Barred from the Bug Hut – you'd be the laughing stock of Paisley. So it doesn't take long before we're all shouting and bawling again. We're fed up waiting, we're dying to get in and see what happens to Buster Crabbe because it's a serial and it always ends up with him in mortal peril, bound hand and foot in an aeroplane maybe that's out of control and divebombing towards a volcano and certain death. Then the screen goes black and it says:

TO BE CONTINUED

And you hear all the weans moaning, Aw fur CHRICE-SAKE!

Or worse.

When at last the checkie lets the rope go there's a big cheer and the weans at the front lead the stampede down the passage and out to the hut at the back where the pictures are on. That's how the Bug Hut got its other name, the Fourpenny Rush. At first I can't figure this out because it's ninepence to get in, but Toono says it's from the old days when it was only fourpence.

But nobody cares about any of this when we're all sitting there in the dark and the big screen lights up and it's Roy Rogers or Johnny Mack Brown, or Frankenstein or Dracula.

I get really feart at the horror pictures because Dracula is always down some dark dungeon hiding in a coffin and the blonde filmstar always goes down there looking for something and you always know she's going to lift the lid of the coffin. And we're all sitting there praying, *Don't dae it, hen, don't stey there, get oot o' there this minnit*, because that's what anybody with any sense would do. But does she listen? No, in the Dracula pictures she always stays and she always opens the lid of the coffin.

What with the dark and the creaky sounds and the filmstar's heavy breathing and the creepy music I'm that feart I'm dying to shut my eyes and cover my ears but I can't because it's only lassies that do that. Then when everything goes dead quiet except for the throbby, echoey music and she stretches out her fingers slow and shaky and touches the coffin my breath sticks in the back of my throat and I'm nearly fainting with the fright. Then somebody shouts:

UR YE THERR DAN?

And the whole place bursts out laughing. The old pensioners get dead annoyed and start hissing *Shoosh! Shoosh!* at us but nobody pays them any heed; we're all that relieved and what do they expect anyway, at a weans' matinée? Nobody knows who started it but it happens nearly every week; at horror pictures or detective pictures, just at the bit where you think the filmstar is going to die and you along with her some boy'll shout out:

UR YE THERR DAN?

Then other boys start shouting back.

NAW, AH'M IN THE LOABBY, BOABBY!

Shoosh!

AH'M UNDER THE TABLE, MABEL!

Shoosh!

AH'M GETTING READY, FREDDY!

AH'M UP THE STREET, PETE!

Shoosh!! That's terrible, so it is! Shoosh!!!

And though sometimes you're not that pleased yourself because it definitely spoils the story, there's other times when you feel it's saved you dying from shock. And the funny thing is, when you're telling your pals about the picture at school on Monday, that's nearly always the bit you remember the best.

I get fed up going the messages, especially when it's all the way up to Well Street because I'd rather be playing bools or football in Galloway Street, or going with Toono and the gang to look for the Lucky Middens.

I try to think up wee games to help me pass the time, though it's hard when all you've got to play with is an empty shopping bag. Sometimes I put my arms through the handles and wear the bag on my back like a rucksack and kid on I'm a lone explorer trekking across the desert or going deep into the Unknown, like the big game hunters in the Tarzan pictures at the Bug Hut, though you can see it's always the same bit of jungle they're going through so you wonder what's Unknown about it. Other times I'm a Creature from Outer Space, like the Mekon in the Dan Dare serials, and the bag over my head is a space helmet or even a giant skull because the creatures from my planet have such big brains. And if I wear the bag on my chest with the straps hooked over my shoulders I can be the drummer in a pipe band or the Orange Walk.

But after a while I get fed up with these games so I

just play football. There's nobody to play with, but I can always kick a wee stone along the pavement in front of me and kid on I'm Charlie Tully at Celtic Park, weaving down the wing with the ball at my feet, beating the lampposts no bother and swerving past the backs and scoring great goals. It's funny, but when there's nobody watching I'm quite good sometimes, I can even do wee tricks; I'm not saying I'm as good as Fatty McKee or anything, mind, but good enough maybe to surprise Big Owen Mangan next time he picks me.

The trouble is, I can only play these games on the way up to Well Street. On the way back I'm nothing but a beast of burden, a pack mule coming down the mountain path dragging my feet home with a loaded shopping bag.

So I come up with the idea of conning my wee brother into taking on the messages in my place. Of course I have to build it up a bit and tell him this is something only big boys can do, a kind of dare or test wee yins have to pass before they can be in the gang.

An' ye hiv tae keep it a secret and no' tell ma mammy, I tell him. Or they'll never let ye in the gang.

It works. Frankie crosses his heart and makes the sign of cutting his throat. He's dead chuffed to get the chance to be in the gang. And for a while after that I have the life o' Riley, as my mammy would say, though of course she's got no idea what I'm up to. She hands me the money, the ration book, the wee list and the empty bag and half an hour later, looking tired but game, I hand her back the full bag with the change. Sometimes, but not very often, if the bag is really heavy she'll give me a penny back for myself. Of course what she doesn't know is that I'm handing the empty bag over to my wee brother at the swings in Brown's Place and then sneaking round to play out the back-doors with my pals until he comes staggering back, lopsided with his load. Sometimes, if I'm feeling generous, I give him one of the bullseyes or dolly mixtures I get with my penny at Jimmy Canning's. But my luck runs out, because Frankie soon gets fed up going the messages for the same reasons I got fed up. What's worse, he twigs that he's doing all the work and getting none of the credit, especially when we still don't let him in the gang.

Aye, he says, Ah bet ma mammy wid like tae know who's *really* been goin' the messages.

This gets me worried. I could be in big trouble here. So I try buttering him up, the way I do with Charlie.

Well Ah must say ye're a fast learner. We wur jist testin' ye. Ah'll tell Toono. Maybe he'll let ye in the gang noo.

He doesn't believe me; I can see it in his face. That's the trouble: he really is a fast learner.

Right, then, I tell him. If you tell ma mammy, ye're for it. Ah'll batter ye, so Ah wull!

That keeps him quiet for a while.

Even so, I'm a bit worried at the way things are going, but then he promises not to say anything if I let him come with me next time I go the messages. I must admit I'm a bit surprised. It looks as if wee brothers will put up with anything rather than get left behind.

I kid on I'm thinking it over.

OK, I say at last. Ye can come wi' me. Ah'll let ye.

I say it as if I'm doing him a big favour, but to tell you the truth I'm glad of the company.

The first time we go up to Well Street together, I start kicking a wee stone in front of me as usual, only this time there's somebody else to play with. We pass the ball back and forth between us, doing backheels and fancy flicks and it's more fun because now when it goes flying into the gutter or gets wedged under a fence, there's two of us to go and get it so we don't waste much time.

But when we're getting up near Well Street it starts to get busy with a lot of people and traffic going past and it's impossible to keep playing. So I pick up our stone and plank it in a corner of some waste-ground.

Frankie doesn't say anything, but I see him watching me with a funny look on his face.

That's jist so we can play wi' the same stane on the way back, I tell him.

On the way back we go and get the same stone and carry on with the game until we're back in Brown's Place and we can see Galbraith's corner. And here I hesitate, because what I do when I'm on my own is hide the stone for the next time. But of course I can't do that in front of Frankie; he'll think I'm a big softie. So I just sort of sidefoot the stone into the gutter, dead gallous, and keep on walking.

Hey, wait a minute, Frankie says. And he goes and gets the stone and planks it under a cigarette packet in a corner near the swings. I can hardly believe what he's doing.

It's nae good plankin' it noo, I scoff at him. We're gaun hame. It'll never be there next time ye look for it.

Frankie looks at me.

Och, Ah know, he says. But that's a good wee stane, intit? It's kept us company hisn't it? So I'm just putting it in there oot o' the rain.

I nearly start jeering at him and calling him a wee

softie but I stop myself in time, because the truth is he's lifted a great weight off my mind.

But that's whit Ah dae! I tell him at last. D'you dae that as well?

I'm dead relieved because I've always felt a bit ashamed about planking a stone because I feel sorry for it, I've always kept it a secret. And now I don't have to any more. I'm not a freak! Other people do the same daft things!

Even when it's only your wee brother, it's a relief to know you're not alone.

It's a photo of a soldier holding a wee baby. The baby has straggly blond hair and a pudgy face. The soldier is smiling. He's got a wee chippoke cap on the side of his head.

The soldier is my daddy. The baby is me.

It's funny because my hair is dark brown, nearly black.

It's true enough, *ahashki*, my mammy says when I ask her. You were pure blond when you were born.

I don't like me in the picture, I look pudgy and grumpy. But it's my daddy's favourite. It's a snap taken when he was back visiting us from the war. In his Army days. It's black and white with a squinty crack down the middle.

Sometimes he shows me different salutes and I have to guess which army.

First he sits up straight though not too stiff and puts his open hand up to the side of his forehead then kind of flicks it down, dead casual.

That's easy. The Yanks.

He does another one, with his hand dead stiff and straight and his thumb beside his ear. I don't know that one.

Irish Free State! he says. He sits up straighter when he says that and looks proud and shy at the same time.

I get the British Army one right away, because that's what he was in during the war even though he's Irish.

Sure didn't I try to tell them that, he says, but they pulled me in jist the same, bad cess to them.

I'm amazed they didn't believe him because you can tell he's Irish dead easy from the way he talks. His mammy and daddy came from Donegal.

But they were over here at the time, he tells me, The pair a them, workin' at the totties. No more than ourselves, God help them. And that's when I was born. Just my bad luck.

Sure we can't choose where we're born, man dear, my mammy says. It's in the hands of the Man Above. And for the love o' God don't always be talking about the totties, she says in her hissy voice. Isn't that all in the past, over and done with?

I don't know what she's got against totties, all of a sudden.

When I ask my daddy what regiment he was in he sits up dead straight and does the British Army salute.

Pioneers, he says.

The Pioneer Core, my mammy sighs. The craitchurs.

I don't know why she says that. I think the Pioneers is a great name. I think of the Far West and the wagon trains and the US cavalry riding in a long column across the prairie. The officers are up in front with their widebrimmed hats and one of them carries the flag fluttering proudly on its pole. My daddy is back with the men in the column because he's not a Bigshot. But he's sitting easy on his horse and holding the reins in one hand. His wee cavalry cap is stuck at a jaunty

94

angle on his head. He's got a Woodbine between his lips and his eyes are screwed up narrow to squint through the prairie dust. They are riding out to save a wagon train from the Cherokees, or a fort surrounded by Apaches. Fearless and proud, the Pioneer Corps gallop towards the far horizon. The dust rises in a cloud behind them and they fade out of sight.

Sometimes when I'm up the street with my mammy, or up in Glasgow at the Barra's, waiting in the crowd to get served at one of the stalls, she'll suddenly grab hold of my arm and pull me closer to her as if she's feart I'll get lost. She does the same thing at the busstop up at Wellmeadow or the Cross, pulls me in and puts her hand on my shoulder, and that's something she never usually does. I think at first it's to keep me back from the kerb in case I get hit by a motor going by.

Whit is it? I ask her. Whit's wrang?

Nothing, she whispers. Nothing at all. Just you stay there, now.

What's she whispering for?

She doesn't look at me, just pulls her coat shut over her chest even though it's buttoned up already, and stares in front of her. She's not looking at anything that I can see. This is different, it's something she doesn't want to look at. I don't know what's wrong; she looks shy and feart at the same time. Then her eyes'll flicker sideyways and I'll notice somebody in the queue, a man that's been watching her, smiling at her, a man we don't know.

Maybe the man's just being friendly, but I don't think so because it's the only time I see my mammy this feart.

It makes me feart as well.

I shuffle closer to her, the way he'll know I'm with
her. He'll know it's two against one.

Eeeelas-ray-ace!
   Eeelas-race feeno-oh!
Most winter nights and especially on Fridays and
Saturdays we'll hear the shouts coming along
Underwood Road.

It's the paperman going to his pitch up at Galbraith's
corner in the fading light with his thick wad of folded
newspapers under his arm. I like to watch the shadows
of his customers coming and going in the lightpuddle
under the lamppost, the way they go wee and fat then
long and skinny, and their breath coming out like
steam from a kettle. Some of the men that buy a paper
stand there for a while squinting at the pages under the
lamppost, then you'll hear them moaning:
Aw fur Chricesake . . . !
Mair bliddy money doon the pan!
And they give the paperman a dirty look when
they're walking away.

Sometimes I stand up there at the edge of the light
and watch him, the way he tugs one paper loose from
the wad with his finger and thumb then kind of flicks
it out with a snap, dead gallous, and collects the coins
in the same hand. He wears a baggy old overcoat and a
bunnet and khaki wool gloves with the fingertops cut
off and every so often he blows into his fist or thumps
himself across the chest with his free arm to warm
himself up, or does a nifty wee shuffle with his feet, as
though he's shadowboxing, and all the heavy coins in
his pockets go *jingle-jangle, jingle-jangle.*
Then he starts shouting again.
Eeelas-ray-ace! Eelas-race Feeno-oh-o!

I'm listening to this for ages but I can never work out what he's saying, so in the end I have to ask Toono, though I don't like to because he can be a bit of a know-all and a show-off sometimes. And it turns out all it means is the Last Race Final, it's the *Evening Times* with the results of the last race so the men can see how they got on with their bets at the bookie's in the afternoon, though how you're supposed to work that out from *Eelasrace Feeno-oh* is a mystery to me.

Sometimes I try and get Barney Molloy to tell me the story of his young days but he never will. He comes up to the house sometimes to visit us. Put it therr, John, he'll say in his slow Donegal way and he sticks out a hand the size of a shovel. When I hold out my hand he gives it a wee squeeze that hurts my fingers but not too much then he lets on to be surprised. Did Ah hurt yer han', John? he says and smiles at me. He's got a wee tash and big yellowy teeth with a gold tip on one of them that flashes sometimes when he talks. When I ask him to tell me about when he was young he only says, Ah now, and sighs and takes a sup at his tea.

'Twas a long time ago. Sure Ah had no sense when Ah was young. Ah had no sense at all till Ah was turty-wan years old.

And I know that's when Mister Molloy took the Pledge though I don't say anything because that's something else we're not supposed to talk about, even though he always wears the wee Pioneer pin in his lapel.

He'll sit there smiling and stirring his tea and not another word out of him. But I know, because my daddy's always telling us the story, that the Molloy brothers were wild men altogether when they were young and one night the three of them, Barney and Owney and Paddy, were arrested for being drunk and fighting at the Hibs Hall and were being taken along Causeyside Street in the paddywagon, though my mammy always butts in here and says God forgive you, man dear, that's a terrible name, it's an insult to the Irish so it is. Can ye not call it by its proper name which is the Black Maria?

Anyway, says my daddy, didn't the Molloys start fighting again inside the van so the two polis driving it had to stop and come round the back to calm them down. And be Jaisus, he says, didn't the Molloys turn on them then, and were too strong for them, and they got away scot-free down them wee streets beside the river Cart.

He gives a wee jerk of his chin to one side as if to say, Would you be up to them Molloys? and sits there with his hands on his knees, smiling into the fire, his eyes shining.

Mister and Missis Molloy live round the corner from us in Underwood Road and the first thing you see when you walk in their house is a big picture of the Sacred Heart above the mantelpiece. But the picture I like to look at is on the wall by the window, a framed certificate in fancy writing with a big red seal at the bottom. It's a certificate for bravery from Paisley Town Hall and Barney Molloy got it for stopping a runaway horse and cart in Causeyside Street one Saturday when it was crowded with people going to the shops. This is the story my mammy likes to tell, how something must have frightened the horse and it bolted away up the street with the cart rattling and bouncing behind it, and people screaming and running about all over the place and Barney just stepped out as cool as you please and jumped up and grabbed onto the reins and hung on round the horse's neck talking to it till it stopped.

Of course it would be no bother to Barney, she'll say. Wasn't he brought up on a farm and used to horses so?

And she'll go back to her ironing, under the dripping pulley at the kitchen table. But I can see from the wee smile on her face that she's proud of Barney Molloy, for didn't he show the world that the Irish and the Catholics can be good for something after all, and we're not all drunkards and wasters the way some people in Paisley like to think?

1950

Before you can receive Holy Communion you have to go to confession and get absolution for your sins so you can be in a State of Grace. You kneel in the church beside all the other sinners on wood kneelers that make your bare knees sore and say prayers while you're waiting your turn to go into the confessional. After you've been kneeling a while it's OK to sit back on the shiny wood pews and when the next sinner goes into the box you all slide along the pew one place till eventually it's your turn. Sometimes the queue moves when you're still kneeling and you have to shuffle sideways on your knees and that's how you get skelfs in them.

When I start going to confessions the hardest thing is thinking of something to confess. The mortal sins are all terrible, like murdering somebody or robbing the bank or missing Sunday Mass without a good excuse. You'll see some old women taking ages to say their penance, saying decades of the Rosary and lighting candles and God knows what else so you know that for all their innocent look they must have committed some terrible mortal sin. The venial sins are lesser sins, it says in the Catechism, like disobedience or telling lies or fighting with your brothers or stealing biscuits out of the press and for a long time this is about all I have to confess. I'm always stealing biscuits out of the press and though I'm sorry afterwards I'm relieved as well because it means at least I've got one sin to tell the priest.

You go into this wee cubicle and when you shut the door behind you it's pitch black sometimes so you can't see a thing and you have to feel down the wall for the wee shelf for your elbows and the kneeler on the floor for your knees. When your eyes get used to the dark you can just about see a wee hatch in front of you and on the other side is the priest. Sometimes he says Yes? or coughs and sometimes he doesn't say anything at all so you're not even sure if he's there but you start anyway. You whisper Bless me Father for I have sinned, it is one week since my last confession. You whisper because you don't want the sinners waiting outside to know your sins.

Yes, my son? says the priest. And that's when you tell him about the lies and the fighting and the stealing biscuits out of the press.

But sometimes I haven't been telling lies or fighting and I haven't even disobeyed my mother or my father or if I did I didn't mean it so it doesn't count. So I have to fall back on my favourite sin.

One time I'm telling Father Murphy about the biscuits and he lets out this big sigh and says, What biscuits are these you're always stealing? Oh, they're rich tea or digestives, Father, I tell him, an' sometimes custard creams. Ah take one out of the press when my mammy isn't looking. Sometimes Ah take two. And he sighs again and says, Listen, son, the press is in your own home and surely your mother got the biscuits for the family to eat, so that's not really stealing, is it now? So you don't have to tell it in confession, all right? Is there anything else? he says.

No, Father.

Very well, son, he says, say one Hail Mary for your penance and go in peace.

When I come out I'm mortified. One Hail Mary is hardly a penance at all, you always get at least three. I get the feeling that Father Murphy is really saying, Don't be wasting my time with your biscuits out of the press when there are real sinners waiting out there who need absolution. And I'm dead worried, wondering what am I going to tell him next week now my favourite sin isn't a sin at all?

Galloway Street is a dead end because of the high railway wall at the bottom of the street. Number fourteen is the last close on our side then there's a wedge of wasteground before you get to the wall, and this is where Davie Leitch from number fourteen parks his lorry. And whenever he pulls out there's always some wean trying to hang onto the back for a hudgie. You wait till he's turned the lorry round so it's facing up the street then you sneak in behind the tailboard and hang on. If you do it right Davie Leitch never knows you're there till you jump off and he sees you in the side mirror and then you'll hear him cursing you out the cab window before the lorry roars away up the street. Effin weans, he shouts. Yeez'll get yersels kilt, ya bliddy wee soansos! Serve yeez right, an' a'! It's scary but it's funny as well because Mister Leitch is usually a quiet man who doesn't say much. And from the day Wee Joe Kerr gets crushed behind his lorry he hardly says a word to anybody.

It seems Wee Joe is hiding behind the lorry when Davie Leitch gets into the cab so he's already hanging onto the back when it's reversing to get out and because Mr Leitch is in a hurry that day or a bad temper he does it too fast and the back of the lorry bangs into the railway wall. And that's how Wee Joe gets his head crushed between the tailboard and the wall. The first we know about it is the ambulance going past our close with the bells clanging and the polis car with the siren howling and when we run down to see we can't get near for the crowd and the polis holding everybody back.

Joe Kerr is the same age as me though we're not really pals because he's a Proddy and supports Rangers and he goes to the North School. But sometimes we're in the same side when we play football in the street and once or twice I've played him at bools or chessies on that same bit of wasteground and we were quite pally then. So when word comes out that he's dead I can hardly believe it. I just keep thinking about the time we buried the pigeon.

It's nighttime and it's dark and me and wee Joe are squatting on our hunkers in the churchyard at the back of Galloway Street with this dead pigeon we're going to bury. It's a pigeon with a broken wing Miss Conlon, my teacher at St James's, found on her balcony where she lives and when she told the class about it I put my hand up and said, Miss, Miss! I know a man in our

102

street who knows about pigeons, maybe he can make it better! I was dead proud when she gave it to me, because I like Miss Conlon, she's got a lovely face. The man's name's Archie Fleming, he lives at number nine and he keeps racing pigeons in a dookit in his backdoor, but I would never have brought Miss Conlon's pigeon to him if I knew what he was going to do to it. Don't worry, son, he says to me, jist you leave it wi' me and Ah'll fix it fur ye. And then as soon as I'm out of sight he goes and wrings its neck. When Wee Joe Kerr tells me this I don't believe him till we sneak through Archie's close later on and find the pigeon in the bin out the backdoor. And that's how Joe and me end up in the churchyard in the dark with the pigeon on the grass between us. It looks terrible with its head twisted to one side and its broken wing all floppy and loose. I don't know what I'm going to say to Miss Conlon. I try to tuck the wing in but it keeps flopping back out.

Should we no' jist bury it here? Joe whispers and I whisper back, Aye, might as well. The truth is I'm a bit feart and I'm dying to get back to the lights in the street, though I don't want Joe to know that. It's creepy out here in the churchyard in the moonlight with the old gravestones leaning this way and that and the trees rustling and their shadows shifting on the side of the church. And though Galloway Street's just behind us we can't even see the lights of the back windows because we're in the shadow of the high dyke we had to climb to get in.

Joe grabs a big clump of grass and starts heaving and tugging and then the whole clod comes loose all at once so he staggers back and lands on his bum. Ya bugger! he says out loud and we're feart somebody *might have heard him, but no, it's all right, there's nobody about.*

The clod's left a goodsized hole and we stick our hands in and scoop out some more dirt to make it bigger.

Right, I say, and I pick up the pigeon and tuck its wing in and I'm getting ready to put it in the hole when Joe says, Wait a minute, ye cannae jist stick it in like that. Should we no' cover it or somethin'?

Oh aye, I say. Right enough. Because a worms 'n that, ye mean? The two of us look scunnered at the notion of worms and we look around for a box or a bit of paper but there's nothing but grass.

Wait a minute, Joe says. Ah've got an idea! And he digs in his pocket and pulls out this big hanky. It's no' very clean, he says. Well, I tell him, It's cleaner than dirt, intit? So we wrap the pigeon up in Joe's hanky and tear up some grass to spread in the hole and I put the bundle on top. Then Joe puts the clod back in the hole and starts ramming it down. Hey, go easy! I say, and Joe says, Oh, right, sorry, and just kinda pats it into place.

Next Joe comes up with the idea of making a wee cross to mark the grave. Ye know, like they dae in the pictures? he says. So's we can come back and visit it, eh? We grope about in the grass for a stick or something we can break to make a cross but all we find is a halfbrick so that has to do as a tombstone.

The day before Joe's funeral word goes round that all his pals are invited up to the Kerrs' house in number fifteen to see him for the last time. And though I'm not really his pal and I'm shy and a bit feart I go up anyway.

By the time I get there there are no other weans left and the room is packed with men and women from Galloway Street and Underwood Road all talking and sighing and shaking their heads and I'm standing there a bit lost when Mister Kerr sees me and comes over with a big tumbler of lemonade. He's a big man with a loud scary voice and a rough manner but now his face has kind of collapsed and I can see he's been greetin'.

D'ye want tae see 'um son? he says and grips my arm and leads me to where a wee white coffin is lying open on a table loaded with flowers and there inside the coffin, framed in white satiny cloth, is Wee Joe, looking all clean and combed and not crushed at all. I am amazed because I know Joe is a scruffy boy with a snottery nose and here he is looking like an angel up in Heaven and him not even a Catholic.

Right, Joe, better get going, eh? I'm up on my feet and ready to go but Joe's still looking down at the grave.

D'ye no' think we should say a wee prayer or somethin'?

I feel ashamed when he says this because it's my pigeon that's dead and here's Joe, and him a Protestant, reminding me it's not a proper funeral unless you say prayers.

Aye, maybe ye're right . . . But what kinda prayers should we say? I'm thinking this could be awkward because we're different religions. Joe doesn't say anything for a while and I wonder if he's thinking the same thing. Then he says, You're a Cathlick, aren't ye?

Aye.

Well, Joe says, it was your pigeon, so maybe ye should say a Cathlick prayer.

Are ye sure?

Yeah, he says in this funny voice. We're buddies, ain't we?

I wonder why he's suddenly started talking like a cowboy in the pictures but I shut my eyes and start saying Hail Marys under my breath, quite fast because I'm dead embarrassed to be saying my prayers in front of a Proddy.

Hail Mary full of grace the Lord is with thee Blessed art thou amongst women and blessed is the fruit of thy wound Jesus Holy Mary Mother o' God pray for us sinners now and at the hour of our death Amen.

I stop after three and open my eyes but Joe's still standing there with his eyes shut, head down, legs apart and his hands crossed in front of his belt as if he's holding a hat or something. You'd think he was Tom Mix or Johnny Mack Brown at the funeral of his best buddy, up there on Boot Hill.

Joe? I say. Are ye all right?

He opens his eyes. Yeah, he says. Okay, buddy, I guess we better make tracks outa here.

We scramble back up the church dyke and sit straddling the top for a while, because just then a long goods train goes rumbling past and makes the dyke shudder under us. We can see the back windows of Galloway Street and quite a few of them are still lit, like wee yellow wafers shining in the black tenement. Thank God for that, I say, the light's still oan in oor hoose. We walk along the top of the dyke and jump down into the wasteground beside the railway wall and come out by the lamppost at the bottom of the street. It's deserted, not a soul anywhere.

Ah better get goin', I say, or Ah'll get murdered.

Joe hasn't said a word since we left the churchyard. He's still away in his wee dream world. He stops in the puddle of light under the lamppost and sticks out his hand, dead sincere, and says Shake, pardner. I can see his eyes shining in the light. I'm a bit embarrassed but I shake hands anyway. Then he puts a finger up to his forehead and flicks me a wee salute, dead gallous, like a cavalryman in the pictures. Adios amigo, he says, and he wheels his horse round and canters away home across the cobbles.

He was a good wee boy, eh son? Mister Kerr says, standing big beside me, and I don't dare to look up at him because I can tell by his choking voice that he's greetin' again. It's the first time I've ever heard a big rough man greetin' and the first time I've ever seen anybody dead, never mind somebody I know, and a great heave of pity comes over me and I feel I should say something serious and grownup for this solemn occasion but I don't know what.

Oh aye, I say. He wis.

Wur yeez good pals, son? Mister Kerr says.

He disnae know my name, I'm thinking. He's probly never even noticed me before. And then I know what I have to say though when I look up into his wrecked face it's hard to talk without greetin' myself.

Mister Kerr, I say at last, Ah wis his best pal.

He looks at me in a puzzled kinda way then his eyes shift down and to the side and I get the feeling he doesn't believe me but doesn't like to say.

Wur ye, son? Is that a fact?

Aye.

Even though it's not true I say it because it feels like the only thing to say. And Mister Kerr just shakes his head dead slow and sad at the queer ways of the world and the two of us stand there looking into the coffin.

Pat comes into work one day wearing one of them lumberjack shirts.

Is that a new shurt ye're wearin'? says Mick.

It is, begod, says Pat. It is indeed. 'Tis a grand shurt altogether.

Is that roight? says Mick.

Ah, says Pat. There's great shtuff in it. Yiss yiss, with this shurt, no matter how cold and wet you are, you're always warm and dry!

Well I don't see what's so funny about that, says my mammy. Isn't it only common sense, wearing good warm clothes in wet weather?

My daddy rolls his eyes up and sighs and looks at me for sympathy.

Honest to God, he says, Ah don't know why Ah bother.

I can see what he means. He comes in tired out from his work and tells a wee joke to cheer us up but my mammy hardly ever gets it. Or else she turns it into something else altogether.

He has a hard life of it at her, right enough.

Is it the night Santa Claus comes? Frankie asks me.

He's all excited. We're sitting out on our landing steps by the back window.

Naw, that's the morra night. Christmas Eve.

We sit out there sometimes and talk. It's freezing but it's always nice and quiet except if somebody comes out to the lavvy then we have to move. There's a broken pane near the top of the window where you can see out. You can't see out anywhere else because it's cloudy glass. It's dark and misty outside but you can still see the sky and a wee slice of moon.

Frankie believes in Santa Claus. He's still a wee boy. I've stopped believing in Santa Claus. I know he doesn't exist, except on Christmas cards and things. Sometimes they write Xmas but Miss Conlon tells us that's a heathen way to spell it and if you spell it like that you might as well be a Protestant. It's called Christmas because it's the Baby Jesus's birthday, she says. The least we can do is spell his name right.

I don't remember who it was that told me about Santa Claus, Porky McNulty maybe, or Danny Deveney. Or Toono. He's a wee bit older than me so he knows things. Big boys always tell wee boys things. It's to help them to grow up and be men. But sometimes I'm sorry they told me, whoever it was. I still like the idea of Santa fat and cheery coming down the chimney with a sackful of toys while his faithful reindeer wait on the roof. You wonder how they keep their balance in the snow on a pointy roof but it's no bother to them. They paw the snow and snuffle through their noses and their breath comes out steamy. I'm a bit jealous of Frankie for still believing in that.

He's telling me what Santa's going to bring him.

The *Beano* annual, a pair a fitba' buits and a pair a woolly gloves.

I'm glad he's getting the *Beano* book because it means I can read it as well. I'm getting the *Oor Wullie* and we can swap. But that's not what I say to him.

D'you still believe in Santa Claus?

He gives me a funny look, suspicious.

How d'ye mean?

D'ye believe a' that aboot Santa and the reindeers 'n' that?

Aye. Sure. D'you no'?

He's trying to sound sure of himself.

Och naw. Santa Claus disnae exist. It's jist a story big people make up to tell their weans.

When I'm saying that I feel a sneery look coming over my face. I feel it round my mouth and jaw.

Frankie's face looks as if somebody slapped it.

Ah don't believe ye. Naw, that's no' true. Who brings us toays at Christmas then?

Ma daddy.

Ma daddy?

Aye.

Is it him that comes doon the lum?

Och don't talk daft! How could he come doon the lum? It's jist kiddin' oan, Ah'm tellin' ye.

He doesn't want to believe me. You can see it in his face.

But Ah saw Santa Claus wance. Wi' ma mammy. At the Coahpurraytuv.

Och that wisnae real. It wis jist a man in a costume.

Wee Johnny McNulty *heard* Santa Claus. That's whit he telt me. It wiz last Christmas. He heard 'um in the kitchen in the middle o' the night.

He keeps arguing. He won't give in.

It must've been Mr McNulty kiddin' oan.

But wee Johnny heard noaises. Bangs and bumps an' things.

It wis probly Mr McNulty bumpin' intae the furniture in the dark. Kiddin' oan. Or mebbe he wis drunk or somethin', how wid Ah know? Ah'm tellin' ye. There's nae such thing as Santa Claus. It's jist a story people tell their weans.

He doesn't say anything. He's thinking. He looks dead worried.

Like fairytales, d'ye mean?

Aye.

His face has gone all crumply the way it does when he's going to start greetin'. Now it's me that's worried because I'll get leathered for spoiling my wee brother's Christmas and making him greet. But it's all right, he holds it in. Then he gives me this look. You can see he wants it to be a dirty look but it comes out pathetic.

Ah wish ye hadnae told me.

I try to cheer him up. I tell him it makes no difference, he'll still get toys and books and things at Christmas. It's just that now he'll know they come from my mammy and daddy, not Santa Claus. He'll know that Santa doesn't exist.

Ye'll be like wan o' the big boays noo, I tell him.

It cheers him up a bit but not much. He doesn't say anything, just keeps staring out the broken pane at the bit of sky. The light on the landing makes his face all pale and sicklooking.

I wish I hadn't told him.

The priest's house is a posh house in Greenock Road near the racecourse, with its own door and a wee garden in the front, and inside it's that quiet all you can hear is the big grandfather clock ticking away in the lobby. The hallway, the woman who lets me in calls it. She's the priest's housekeeper and she's very well spoken, as my mammy would say.

It's Saturday morning and I'm sitting on the couch with Pat Foley and Hughie McDowall from my class, and we're all dead proud because we've been picked to be altarboys.

Father Murphy's a tall thin priest with a nice face but a very serious manner, though today he's smiling and a lot friendlier than he ever looks on the altar. He hands us out cards with the Latin of the Mass in thick black print and the English words in ordinary print underneath.

Introibo ad altare deus, it says in black. That's the priest's bit, Father Murphy says, and it means I shall go unto the altar of God. Then it's the altarboy's response *Ad deum qui laetificat juventutem meam* – to God who brings joy to my youth.

It's dead hard because we've never seen Latin words before and to be honest even the English words sound odd to us. And we have to learn all this Latin by heart before we can be altarboys because the cards are just for learners. You're not supposed to use them on the altar. But Father Murphy tells us we have a few more Saturday mornings ahead of us yet and he teaches us how to pronounce the words and after a while we start to get the hang of it.

Then we get to the *Confiteor*, which means I confess, and this is a very holy bit of the Mass where we have to bow down low and beat our breasts and say *Mea culpa, mea culpa, mea maxima culpa*. That means Through my fault, Through my fault, Through my most grievous fault. But then Father Murphy says to Foley, Go easy there, Patrick. You're supposed to be beating your breast, not punching yourself in the stomach, and we all burst out laughing. And Father Murphy's laughing as well, so it's OK. Then he teaches us a wee trick to help us remember the words, though we're to promise never to tell anybody he told us this, especially Father O'Sullivan the Parish Priest because, Father Murphy says, You don't want to get me into trouble with the Boss, do you? Anyway, he says, here's the trick: just think of it as *Me a cowboy, Me a cowboy, Me a Mexican cowboy*. We all think this is great.

But, he says, for Heaven's sake don't get mixed up

112

when you're serving Mass and come out with that instead. That would never do, he says, especially if it's Father O'Sullivan that's saying Mass that day.

In the cowboy pictures we see at the Bug Hut or the Palladium – the Palla-doodyum Toono calls it – the cowboy always gets to kiss the lady near the end and we all start groaning and fidgeting because we want it to get back to the shooting and the fighting and the fast draw contests in the saloon or out in the dust in the main street. The kissing is exciting as well, in a way, though I'd never tell any of my pals this. Watching the kissing on the screen makes me embarrassed but at the same time I get a funny tingly feeling, as if it's me kissing Elizabeth McNally or May Kane. Sometimes at night I lie in bed thinking about these things before I go to sleep or if I get woken up by the trains going by at the end of the street.

I think about a woman with a really beautiful face that I've seen during the day, like Miss Conlon at school maybe, and I shut my eyes and imagine her kissing the cowboy so I can get the tingly feeling. When I'm walking home from school or sitting on the bus I pick out a lady with a nice face and think to myself, You can be the one kissing the cowboy tonight. Then one night I get a better idea, I imagine it's me she's kissing instead of the cowboy. And this is the best of all. I'm not even feart of the dark the way I am sometimes, I'm all warm and tingly lying in bed kissing a beautiful lady.

> Fay-haith of our Fa-hah-theh-ers
> Li-ving still
> In – spite – of Dungeonfireandsword!

113

I'm standing next to my daddy at Mass at St James's Church, though it's not a real church at all, my mammy says, only a converted old mill on the river Cart and isn't it a shame what the Catholics have to put up with in this pagan country.

We're singing 'Faith of our Fathers', which is one of our favourite hymns.

I always get a wee kinda tingle when I'm singing *Dungeonfireandsword* and when we come to the chorus, the bit about being True to Thee till Death, my daddy always throws back his head and sings louder because that's his favourite bit. But this day I notice he's not singing Thee till Death at all, he's singing different words, something like Deedle Dell. So I don't sing so loud myself next time round and I listen hard and right enough he's singing Deedle Dell instead of Thee Till Death. I'm mortified in case the people standing near us might hear him. Sometimes I'm a bit ashamed of my daddy, to tell the God's honest truth, because he can't read properly and he sits there with his mouth open whispering the words to himself like a dunce at school. And he talks different from the other men in Galloway Street, kinda Irish and slow, and he's got daft ways of saying things sometimes, like numberella instead of umbrella or rubbage instead of rubbish, and lets us down altogether.

I'm trying to think of some way of talking to him about this Deedle Dell so when we're walking home I say to him, Daddy, Ah really like that hymn, that Faith of our Fathers, dae you?

Oh aye, son, he says, Sure that's my favourite.

He smiles.

Ah love that wee bit about Deedle Dell.

And the next thing I know he's throwing his head

back and shaking it from side to side the way he does
and singing

> *We-Will*
> *Be True to Deedle-Dell!*
> *We-Will*
> *Be True to Deedle-Dell!*

Thank God he's only singing under his breath
because we're out in the street but Oh my God, I'm
thinking, he really does think it's Deedle Dell. What'll
people say if they hear him? He'll shame us all.

I have to do something.

Deedle Dell? I say. Is that what it is, Daddy? That's
funny, Ah always thought it was Thee Till Death. Ye
know? We will be true to Thee Till Death . . .

Och away ye go, he says. What do you know about
it? I've been singing that hymn for years, sure I know it
backways. It's Deedle Dell all right, believe me.

But are ye sure? I ask him. I mean, Thee Till Death
wid make mair sense, wid it no'? We will be true to
Thee Till—

I stop because he suddenly turns on me and looks at
me the way he does when he's in a rage, with his eyes
rolling up and half shut so you can only see the white
bits.

Are you tellin' yer daddy what to do? he hisses at
me. By Jaisus, don't I get enough o' that at me work
without you startin'. Now shut yer gob and don't be
bothering me, d'ye hear?

We walk all the way home without talking and I'm
miserable because he's angry at me but I'm still saying
a wee prayer in my head that he won't shame us
all with his Deedle Dell. And the next Sunday I'm

115

standing beside him at Mass and when the time comes to sing 'Faith of our Fathers' I notice he's not singing the chorus louder the way he usually does, in fact I have to strain to hear him at all, but I'm pretty sure he's singing Thee Till Death. Thank God for that, I'm thinking, what a relief, though when I sneak a wee look sideyways up at my daddy I feel bad because I can see he's not enjoying it the way he used to.

Miss Conlon's gone out of the class and some of us are firing folded milktops at each other with elastic slings and I get Charlie Miller in the dunces' row right in the ear. And Pat Foley and Jim McColl who sit near me in the clever row have a good laugh at Charlie when he claps his hand to his ear and jumps up howling. But when he turns round and sees us laughing he takes it in earnest and says Ah'm gonnae get you fur that, Boyle. And though I'm still laughing my heart's not in it. Aw come on, Charlie, I say, it wiz jist in fun. But he only glares at me. Ah've goat an abscess in that ear, he says. You're for it, Boyle. Efter school, right?

It's true that Charlie was off school for nearly a week and had a bandage on his ear when he came back but I think what gets him is the way Foley and McColl are laughing and jeering. It's all right for them, they're not the ones that have to fight him after school.

Ye're no feart o' *him* are ye? Foley scoffs.

Who, me? Naw, I say, because what else can you say in front of a pair of jeerers like McColl and Foley? But the truth is I've always been a bit feart of Charlie. We both live in Galloway Street and I've seen him fighting there and I know he'd murder me.

And Charlie knows it as well. I can see from the way he looks at me.

Right, he says, and gives me a wee nod. See ye efter school, then.

He looks dead sure of himself and all afternoon I've got no idea what Miss Conlon is talking about because I'm dying in my stomach with the fear. But I have to act casual because McColl's behind me whispering that it's got to be proper boxing with rounds and seconds out and he wants to be my second and so does Foley. In fact when word gets round the class nearly everybody's on my side, hardly anybody supports Charlie because he's a dunce with a snottery nose and talks wheezy because of his asthma and all the smart alecs laugh at him behind his back.

I've been serving Mass that morning so I've got my black altarboy sandshoes in my haversack and because it's to be a proper boxing match I think I'll wear them to be light on my feet and maybe have a better chance. Foley's an altarboy as well and he's shocked. Ye cannae wear yer altar shoes fur a fight, he says, That's a sin, but sin or no sin I'm still wearing them because I need all the help I can get.

When we get down to the wasteground near the burn at the back of the school, there's a big crowd of boys waiting. It's freezing and misty and the light is fading so the breath comes out of your mouth like wee smoke signals. Most of the crowd are round me and Charlie is standing a bit away from us with Owen Mangan and Tommy Duignan. They're to be his seconds, but only because nobody else wanted to.

Charlie's got this wee sickly grin on his face. I think he's embarrassed because nearly everybody's on my side. But no matter how bad he feels he's feeling better than me because he knows that once it starts it's going to be just between the two of us.

117

McColl has seen all these American pictures and he's taking it all dead serious so he shouts Seconds Out and the fight is on. And though I've got no chance I go out like a knight of old determined to meet my doom with honour in the field of battle and not be shamed in front of my pals. I don't know how I make it through the first round. I'm a bit taller than Charlie and skipping about on my altarboy sandshoes I manage to dodge most of his punches, which are real haymakers and put the fear of God into me. In fact I land one good one myself right on his sore ear just as McColl goes Drrongg! for the end of the round and I see Charlie flinch with the pain. But when I turn to go back to my corner I feel this tremendous thump in the back and I stagger and nearly fall, and I've got Charlie's strangled breathing in my ear and his slavers and snotters all over my neck because he's jumped me from behind and OhmyGod, I'm thinking, Ah've had it, he'll murder me, because I've seen Charlie fighting mad like this before. But McColl and Foley haul him off me and McColl shouts, Back to yer coarner, Miller, it's supposed to be a square go! And thanks be to God and St Jude, who Miss Conlon says is the patron saint of hopeless cases and the only man for the likes of us, Charlie only scowls at me and walks away.

Use your reach, Johnny boy, McColl's saying and Foley's telling me Go in for the kill and watch his right hook, and thank God they're that busy rubbing my shoulders and talking out of the side of their mouths like tough guys in the pictures they don't notice I'm shaking with fear. My only chance is to hit Charlie again on his sore ear. Go for his ear, I keep saying to myself, Go for his ear. When we go out for the second round Charlie is crouched there waiting for me to start skipping about like I did in the first but instead I rush across and nail him as hard as I can on his bad ear. And he bends down holding his ear and I can see he's in agony and though it's not fair and I even feel a bit sorry for Charlie I steady myself and swing my fist again as hard as I can right into his face.

I hit him that hard it skins my knuckles and Charlie lets out a wee kinda moan and drops to one knee and though he's got one hand on his ear and the other clapped over his eye I'm that feart I'm getting ready to punch him again when McColl runs out and yanks up my fist and shouts The Champ! And though Charlie's back on his feet he's still hunched up and covering his face so I know it's finished.

Everybody is thumping me on the back and calling me Champ but when I see Charlie standing on his own with his hand still clapped to his ear I'm ashamed. So he's the one I end up walking home with because we're pals from Galloway Street and to tell the truth I like Charlie better than McColl or Foley or the rest of them. Anyway I want to keep in with him because I know in my heart that in a real fight he would beat the bejesus out of me.

My daddy's Celtic daft. The bhoys in green, he calls them.

The Celtic strip's green and white. Rangers' is blue.

Green's a better colour, my daddy says. Green is God's colour. The grass is green, the trees is green. Everything that grows on the face o' the earth is green.

But the sky's blue, intit? I ask him.

Och, well, he says, and you can see he doesn't like me saying that. Then he looks up at the sky and laughs.

119

No' the day, though, eh? Like a durty oul' dishcloth, more like it.

He's right enough. It cheers him up. He's laughing away.

Aye, ye have to admit, the sky's no' blue very often roun' here, is it now?

But whit aboot the sea, Daddy? The sea's blue.

Ach away ye go, he says. The sea's oney blue in them Hollywood pitchers. The sea's really green. When ye're in the watter, the sea's green.

I've hardly ever seen the sea. The last time was when we went on a bus run to Saltcoats. It was raining and the sea was flat and grey, like a big slab of wet pavement.

Anyway it's no good arguing with him. Green's the greatest colour in the world and that's all about it.

But when he takes me to the football it's nearly always Love Street, to see St Mirren. We hardly ever go to Parkhead to watch Celtic because my mammy won't let us.

Arra ye'll do no such thing, she says. Ye wouldn't be that foolish, surely? Isn't St Mirren the Paisley team? Aren't you better off going supporting them, isn't it easier and cheaper and a lot safer too, the Lord save us, instead of trailing the child up to Glasgow and mixing with them latchykos at Celtic and Rangers? They're like wild beasts, God help us, the one lot as bad as the other, roaring and fighting half the time. And it's no wonder, the way their heads are destroyed with the drink. Ye'll be as bad yerself if ye carry on the way ye're going, the signs'll be by ye.

I think that last bit's meant for my daddy, not me. She's always moaning about him spending his wages in the pub and coming home drunk.

So my daddy doesn't take me to the football very often, because we can't afford it, and when he does it's nearly always Love Street.

Annythin' for a quiet life, he says, tossing his head back and rolling his eyes up. Sure Ah'd never hear the last o' it if Ah took ye up to Parkhead.

But Love Street's great, too. I love the way the queues narrow down to go through the turnstiles so you have to squeeze through the wee barrier one at a time, block then turn, block then turn, like when you're winding the big clock on the mantelpiece.

My daddy always tries to lift me over to save money.

Is it all right if Ah lift the wee boy over? he says to the man in his shy way.

If the man says Aye it's all right he lifts me up so my feet skliff the top bar then lets me down the other side. I get a bit dizzy when I'm up there but it feels great.

But sometimes the answer's no and he has to pay for me as well and then he'll be moaning all the way up the wide steps.

Miserable oul' bugger that fella, eh? Did ye see the gob on him? I bet ye he wis a Bluenose. Begod, ye'd think it was a crime, askin' to let a chile in for nothin' . . .

He whispers the bit about the Bluenose in case anybody hears us but I'm only half listening, I'm that excited by all the noise and the crowds. I'm surrounded by dark trouserlegs and boots tramping and scuffling up the steps because the game's nearly starting; I have to hold on tight to my daddy's hand in case I fall and get trampled to death. As we get near the top I can hear the roar of the crowd that's already in getting louder and louder. Then we come over the top at the back and the noise hits us that hard it knocks

121

the breath out of me. It's like teetering on the rim of a giant bowl: the terraces spread out below us are that steep it makes me dizzy and they're jampacked and heaving with thousands of St Mirren supporters in their bunnets and scarves and rosettes, *blackandwhiteandblackandwhiteandblackandwhite* like waves in the wind, and a long way past them, all the way down, is the pitch, floating out there in the middle like a magic island of shining, perfect green.

I'm invited to May Kane's party! May Kane's quite clever, she sits up near the front of the lassies' row. She's very nicelooking, with short black flicky hair and blue eyes. To tell the truth, I love May Kane and I think maybe she knows because sometimes I catch her looking at me. She looks away but then turns back with a flick of her hair and gives me a cheeky wee smile. Her hair's jet black and her eyes are brilliant blue.

May Kane? says my mammy when I tell her. The Lord save us, what kind o' a name's that?

She's always saying things like that. The next thing is, she doesn't want to give me money for a present.

Why should I go shelling out for a present, she says, when I don't know the girl from Adam? We've got better things to do than buy presents for flippertigibbets, believe me.

Flippertigibbets. I get the feeling she knows I really want to go to this party and that's why she's trying to put me off. She just doesn't like the sound of May Kane, and that's that.

Eventually I get some money off her for a wee present and I'm ready to go. But when the time comes it's a cold night with ice on the roads and she says it's too cold and slippy and I better stay at home. I'm desperate, because I know if I don't go to this party I'll miss my chance with May Kane. In the end she says OK, I can go, but I have to wear this horrible hairy tweed coat she bought secondhand somewhere. She's always buying me secondhand stuff. Frankie's always moaning if he gets my old clothes but at least he knows who had them before him: I've got no idea where mine come from.

Anyway this tweed coat is too big for me, as usual — Ye'll grow into it, she says, as usual — but what I really hate is the colour. It's supposed to be tan but it's this orangy colour, in fact it makes me look like an orang-utan. I never wear it, I'd rather freeze to death. But this night I have to, or she won't let me out of the house.

On the bus I get the feeling everybody's looking at me in this daft orange coat but I'm hoping it won't be too bad when I get to May Kane's house. It'll be dark outside and I can take it off as soon as I get in.

Oh so *you're* John, her mother says when she opens the door and I tell her my name. I get the feeling May Kane's been telling her about me, because she keeps me there talking in the lobby, in the light, and me still wearing this horrible coat.

When at last I can take it off a neighbour who's there helping shows me where to put it, in a wee room near the front door.

That's a nice coat, she says to Mrs Kane, as she lays it on top of the pile on the bed. It's very unusual, isn't it?

Oh it is, indeed, says Mrs Kane.

She's very well spoken, as my mammy would say.

Where did you get it, son?

Oh ma mammy bought it for me, up the high street somewhere, the Coahpurr-aytiv probly.

Of course I know my mammy went nowhere near the Co-operative, she got it secondhand up at the Barra's maybe; she's up there nearly every week. I'm dying with embarrassment, I can hardly wait to get out of there.

But when Mrs Kane tells me to go in and join the party, she's still standing with the other woman looking at the coat and they're whispering about something. I hear bits of what they're saying:

Is that no' . . . ?

It looks very like . . .

That's what Ah thought . . .

They look up and see me still standing there listening and Mrs Kane just laughs but it sounds a bit forced.

On ye go then, she says. It's in the living room. Don't be shy!

She definitely sounds different now. As if she's laughing at me.

I go out into the lobby and I can hear shouts and laughing coming from the living room. Behind me in the wee room the two women are still whispering.

What are they saying?

I get the feeling they must've seen that coat somewhere before. Maybe they even know who had it before me. They *know* it's secondhand.

I'm mortified. I feel like sneaking back out the front door and going straight home. But I can't leave the coat behind, my mammy would murder me. And how could I face May Kane at school in the morning?

I feel trapped, nowhere to hide. I just stand there in the lobby outside the living-room door. I have to concentrate hard to make my face look normal. Then I push the door open and go into the party.

It's always cold and damp in the lavvy on the landing. It's got a broken wooden seat that wobbles and gets wet sometimes where somebody's peed and missed the pan. The door is thick old wood with cracks and knot-holes in it but you can't really see in to spy, not unless you're Keyhole Kate or Nosy Parker. There's a big iron lock and key and you have to make sure you lock it when you're doing a number two in case somebody comes in. As soon as I hear footsteps on the stairs I shout, Somebody's in! because I'm that feart they might open the door and me with my trousers down and my wullie showing and my bum all bare. I think that must be the worst thing that could happen to you. Sometimes the lock's not working or the key's missing and I nearly fall off the seat stretching out to hold the door shut.

There's paper hanging up on a nail or lying soggy on the floor. Usually it's the *Paisley Express* or the *Daily Record* and they're not bad because you've got something to read when you're on the pan and it's not too sore when you wipe your bum. But sometimes there's only brown paper or that shiny paper you get in the magazines my mammy reads, *Woman* or *Woman's Own*. That's horrible, hard paper, it gets all pointy when you fold it and it's dead sore. And it's slippy as well so you can't even clean yourself right and then you get dirty marks on your pants.

Sometimes there's no paper at all and I have to run back up the stairs to get some even if I'm bursting. The worst is when you don't notice there's no paper until you're nearly finished. That's you stuck there shouting till somebody brings you paper and then you have to take what you get even if it's that glossy stuff.

One time Frankie brought me down strips of wall-paper. He was in a huff with me because I'd skelped his ear for giving me lip out in the street.

At St James's one day Foley and McColl ask me a riddle they got out of the *Sunday Post.*

Whit's four inches wide and a hundred feet long but can fit easy in the wee-est room in the hoose?

I try to work it out but I can't.

The toilet roll! they shout, dead chuffed I didn't get it.

I still don't get it.

Whit's the toilet roll?

They give each other a look then McColl says, The lavvy paper, ya mug ye!

I don't see what lavvy paper has got to do with rolls. Rolls are for eating. I'm just going to say that when I see they're looking at me funny.

So I kid on I get it.

Oh aye, right, I say, and I slap myself on the fore-head.

Whit's wrang wi' me, am Ah daft or whit?

It works. They still jeer at me but then they start talking about something else.

I'm dead worried. Is this something everybody knows about except me?

I ask my mammy.

A lot of oul' nonsense, that's all it is, she says. A waste of good money.

She says that about nearly everything. I keep pestering her.

Ah it's a roll of special paper for wiping your back-side, supposed to be. Did you ever hear the like of it? Paying out good money for a thing like that.

When she tells me this I realize I've seen a toilet roll.

It was the time Father Murphy took all the altarboys from St James's Church out to a fancy restaurant in Glasgow. When I had to go to the lavvy I couldn't believe the luxury. The mirrors, the lovely tiles on the walls and a row of spotless washhand basins. I was shocked to see the dirty words and drawings on the back of the lavvy door but I read them anyway, I couldn't help it. When I was finished I looked for bits of newspaper to wipe myself but couldn't see any. Then I saw this wee roller thing on the wall with paper on it that soft it was like cloth. I could hardly believe you were supposed to use this nice paper for wiping your bum. I had to use it because I couldn't see anything else but I never told anybody about it in case I'd made a terrible mistake.

When my mammy explains to me about toilet rolls I realize there's things my pals at school know but I don't. Things they've got we haven't got. Words they know that we don't. It makes me jealous and ashamed. How come our family always has to be different? How can we never just be ordinary like other people?

On Saturday nights after he's checked his coupon my daddy likes listening to the Scottish Dance Music on the wireless. The band he likes best is Jimmy Shand and His Band. If they announce somebody else, like Bobby McLeod and His Band, he tuts and jerks his head back and rolls his eyes up.

Ach, he says, who wants tae listen to that oul' rubbage?

But then he listens just the same, sitting by the fire with his head to one side and his eyes shut and one ankle crossed over the other and his two feet twitching. I quite like the music myself though I can never tell the

127

difference between one band and the other. But he always knows when it's Jimmy Shand.

Bejaisus, he says, that's a great band altogether. Ah, them's the bhoys can play.

And he'll take a long drag on his Woodbine and sigh, and you can see the firelight dancing in his watery eyes.

The wireless we've got is a tall one in old polished wood my mammy got secondhand from someplace up the town — It's walnut, she says, the real McCoy — and the wood's cut into a pattern like tree trunks over a panel of sackcloth in the middle where the sound comes out, like the wee square of curtain the priest talks through in the confessional.

This is the BBC Light Programme, the posh voice says, or

This is the BBC Home Service . . . Here is the news . . .

The names of the programmes are on a wee dial with a whiskycoloured light glowing behind it. Sometimes when I'm on my own I twiddle the knob so the needle goes to places on the dial with foreign names, like Hilversum or Berlin or Marseilles or Prague. I like listening to the foreign languages, though I can't make head nor tail of them, especially when you get these whistling, screechy noises like messages in Morse Code coming from outer space. The trouble with our wireless is, it sometimes does this when we're only listening to the BBC.

Interference, my daddy calls it.

Arra the curse o' Christ on it, he says when it happens during the football results. God forgive me, he says.

He fills in his coupon every week. He does the

Treble Chance and sometimes the Four Aways. Sometimes he lets me sit beside him at the kitchen table under the pulley and look at the list of teams. I love the way the man on the wireless says the names, especially Hamilton Academicals and Queen of the South and Heart of Midlothian. People usually just call them Hearts, though; it's a shame.

The Four Aways are the best because you get a better chance, at least so Toono says.

Ye only hiv tae pick four teams ye think ur gonnae win away fae hame. Compairt tae the treble chance it's a doddle.

He's right enough. In the treble chance you have to pick eight games that are going to be a draw. But when I try to pass on Toono's tip my daddy just gets angry.

Ach away ye go, he says, sure what does he know about it, a wee nyaff like him?

But I notice he always fills in the Four Aways after that.

Sometimes when he's sitting a big drip from the washing on the pulley will splash right in the middle of the Treble Chance and make the ink all runny.

Arra sufferin' duck, says my daddy. What kine o' a house is this? Big drops of watther comin' down on yer head. Look at that, me coupon's ruined. Is there no place a man can sit down an' do his pools in peace?

He fills in the coupon every week because he's hoping to win a thousand pounds so we can go to Canada, like the people from number nine who won the *News of the World* Prize Crossword. Or even Australia's sunny shore, like the Wild Colonial Boy.

We won the Four Aways once. It was dead exciting, getting the first three right then waiting for the fourth.

Doncaster 1 . . . said the man on the wireless.

And the two of us went mad altogether, jumping around the kitchen and my daddy laughing that hard he was nearly greetin'. We couldn't believe it. But it was right enough, we checked it in the *Sunday Post* the next day.

So my daddy sends in his claim and that's us for the rest of the week, imagining what it'll be like to be rich in Canada or Australia.

Ah now, hold yer horses, my mammy keeps saying, it's only the Four Aways. I doubt ye'll get much even if ye did win.

Arra what do you know about it? says my daddy.

But we can see she's excited all the same, because even if it's not a thousand pounds it's bound to be a few hundred.

When the postman comes at last she shuts the door behind him and tears the envelope open.

It's a cheque for seven shillings and sixpence.

It seems the Four Aways was that easy that week there were thousands of winners instead of two or three.

Seven and six. What a swindle.

But my daddy still keeps filling in the coupon every week and listening to the results on the wireless on Saturday night, and he gets as worked up and excited as ever.

That's why he goes mad when the screeching sounds start.

Sufferin' duck, he says. What kine o' a bliddy wireless is that at all?

Ah for the love o' God, man dear, says my mammy when it's *Family Favourites* we're listening to on a Sunday morning, can ye not do something with that wireless?

It's the valves, he says, nodding. It's the valves is jiggered on it.

The way he says this and talks about interference you'd think he knows what's wrong with it, but when he turns it round and looks in the back all he does is sit there tutting and shaking his head and poking at these big bulbs glowing among the wires and damn the bit of good does it do as far as I can see, especially when I'm trying to listen to *Dick Barton, Special Agent*.

Arra watch what you're doing, for the love o' God, says my mammy, and you can tell by her voice she's getting fed up. D'ye want to electrocute yourself, or what?

At least that's what she says. What she means is, Arra leave the bliddy thing alone, ye're only making it worse.

One night he figures out that if you keep your finger pressed down on the top of the middle valve, the buzzing and screeching stops and you can hear the programme no bother. The trouble is, nothing else seems to work. He tries leaning a spoon on it, then a book; he even balances the salt cellar on it, jammed in against the back of the set, but it's no good. The whining and screeching only gets worse.

Would ye believe that? says my mammy. It's the personal touch that's needed, *ahashki*, nothing else will do.

Guess who gets the job of sitting next to the wireless with his finger on the valve whenever they want to listen to something?

At first our visitors are a bit embarrassed watching me sitting there with my hand stuck in the back while they're listening, then they get used to it and after a while they stop passing remarks altogether, in fact

131

sometimes I wonder if they even notice I'm there.

I'm stuck there one night when my Uncle John and my Auntie Bradley and Old Jimmy Bradley are visiting and we're all listening to a story from *The Man in Black*, Valentine Dyall. It's the creepiest story I've ever heard and the man tells it in this scary voice and the music playing in the background would frighten the life out of you, the way it does in the Dracula pictures at the Astoria, except here there's nobody to shout *Urr ye therr Dan?* to make us laugh and break the suspense.

There was a powerful presence in that dim room, says Valentine Dyall. *Although it was empty, somehow I could sense that I was not alone.*

Even though we're all sitting there with the lights on it's dead scary the way everybody is leaning in and listening, and nobody daring to say a word.

My eye was drawn to a square flagstone in one corner of the floor. I crouched to examine it more closely. A rusty iron ring was set into a small recess in the middle. Slowly, with mounting dread, I stretched out my hand and grasped . . .

THE SCREECHY FIDDLE MUSIC GETS LOUDER, LIKE A SCREAM STARTING IN SLOW MOTION.

If I was the only one listening I'd have switched off the wireless long ago. In fact I'm that feart I nearly take my finger off the valve, but I don't dare. I can't move, I can hardly breathe. I just have to sit there and listen.

Slowly, warily, I raised the heavy flagstone . . .

GRATING SOUND OF THE TRAPDOOR OPENING. THE MUSIC QUIVERS.

I looked down into pitch blackness, as if I were peering down into a well. Into nothingness. Into the pit of hell. Then slowly, as in a trance of terror, I saw what looked like human eyes floating up towards me . . .

THE MUSIC RISES TO A HIGH PITCHED SCREAM AND VIBRATES.

And thanks be to God that's the end of the episode.

Good ga-God all-ma-mighty, says my Uncle John. That man tells a pa-powerful story.

By God he does, says Old Jimmy Bradley. He does surely. We'll have to be sure and listen to that agin next week.

For once in my life I'm pleased to get to my bed, for all the good it does me, because that night and for months after it I have a terrible dream about eyes floating up from pitch blackness and my head hammering with the rhythm of a train that's howling towards me out of another dream.

I'm in the vestry at St James's watching Father Murphy getting ready for the eight o'clock Mass. I've already changed into my black soutane and surplice and lit the candles on the altar. At this hour the vestry is still chilly and dim, except for two wee candles burning in red glass bowls on the dark dresser. The vestments are kept in the bottom half, an immense old-fashioned chest of drawers in dark polished wood with gleaming brass handles, and a set of shelves and drawers above it. It's the biggest, richest furniture I've ever seen; it would never fit in our kitchen, you'd never even get it through the door. It belongs in an old castle some-where, like Hereward the Wake's.

The drawers where the vestments are kept are wide but not deep, more like heavy trays than drawers. Still in his black soutane Father Murphy slides one open and lifts out the creamy white alb on the open palms of his hands and lays it on the flat polished wood. Then he slides the drawer shut again; it makes a

133

smooth, heavy, rich sound. He opens out the alb and slips it on over his head, over his soutane. When the gown falls in folds down around his body he ties it at the waist with the thick white pleated cord they use for a belt. He ties it a special way so the extra cord hangs down in a nice pattern, and he checks it in a long dark framed glass that stands tilted in the corner and reflects the candleflames. Then he slides open another drawer and lifts out the chasuble. Today it's the shiny green one embroidered with a gold cross. That's my favourite because it's like the Celtic colours, though I'd never say that to Father Murphy. He can be funny about these things.

Watching Father Murphy when he's getting ready to say Mass like this I never dare to talk to him. He's that quiet and serious you'd think he was up on the altar in front of the congregation at Sunday Mass, not in an empty vestry on a cold weekday morning with just one sleepy altarboy watching him. Watching his handsome, holy face when he's sliding the heavy wood drawers open and shut, putting on the rich robes, then bowing down over the polished surface of the dresser and muttering a wee prayer to himself before we go out onto the altar, I think it must be great to be a priest. Imagine being surrounded by this peace and quiet and holiness always, instead of weans shouting and greetin' in the closes and their mammies and daddies arguing, the way things are in Galloway Street most of the time.

Watching Father Murphy in this holy place, I think I would like to be him.

My auntie Mary in Preston's had news of Poor Pat. An Achill man was in a pub in London and he saw a fella walking past the door that was the spit of Pat Sweeney.

He went outside to look but the fella was gone.

Well, good for Pat, says my mammy, if it was him at all, the craitchur. Walking past the pub, I mean. By God, he'll not go far wrong if he keeps that up.

My daddy looks over at me for sympathy and rolls his eyes. He's trying to make me laugh, but I don't.

I just kid on I'm concentrating on my comic.

My daddy's manners at the table are terrible. He can't help it, I suppose, he left school when he was twelve and had to go out working the land with his daddy so he never got a proper education. And his nose is all bashed and bent from fights in the pub when he was a young man so he can't breathe right. It always sounds as if he's got a cold, with all the wheezing and whistling noises he makes.

He's only a labourer and he has to work outside in all weathers, in the muck and the wet, so sometimes you feel a bit sorry for him. But it can be a dead scunner when you're trying to eat your dinner.

The worst of all is the wintertime when we're getting soup. I like soup, especially lentil or barley or split pea, but my daddy puts me right off it. He'll come in from his work shivering with the cold and clearing his throat then sniffing it all back and swallowing it.

Then he sits down with us and starts slurping his soup.

I try my hardest not to watch him or listen to him but I can't help it. He sits there with the breath wheezing and whistling through his nose. Can he not hear himself? I wonder. What's worse, the hairs in his nose get all wet and shiny and soon there's a big drop dangling at the tip of it. It could plop into his soup any minute. But he doesn't seem to know and I don't dare to tell him.

135

You can't talk to him nowadays. If I try to tell him anything or give him a wee bit of advice now and again he gets raging mad and jumps down my throat.

He picks up his spoon and scrapes it along the bottom of his plate, then lifts it to his mouth and blows it to cool the soup, then he sooks it up.

Hhh-pwhoooh! Sschlooop!

That's how it goes on, all the way through our dinner.

Sniff! Sniff! Gloop.

Scr-rape.

Hhh-phwhoooh!

Ssschlooop!

I look around at my mammy and Margaret and Frankie, to see how they're taking it. It's no use looking at baby Vincent; he's nearly as bad as my daddy.

By the look of them, they're not bothered at all. I wonder if they've even noticed anything. They're all sitting there quite the thing, eating their soup, and not a word or a funny look out of them.

Sometimes I wonder if I belong to this family. Maybe there was some terrible mix-up at Barshaw Park.

Give her her due, my mammy hardly makes any noise with her spoon. She never sniffs and if she does she always dabs her nose with a wee hanky she keeps in her apron. Sometimes she complains to me about my daddy, as much as to say that she was a cut above him and it was a sad day for her the day she married him. I feel rotten when she says that because if she hadn't married him, I wouldn't even be alive. And I feel sorry for my daddy because it's not fair her telling me these things behind his back.

But sometimes I have to admit I can see what she means.

136

I sneak a wee look at him.

The bead on the tip of his nose has disappeared. It must've fallen into his soup. Just thinking about it makes me shudder. I nearly feel sick.

But he's not bothered, slurping and wheezing away.

Scrrrape. Hhh-phwhoooh! Ssschlooop!

What ye don't know won't hurt ye, he always says.

It's all right for him, he can't see himself.

Another wee bead is starting to form on his nose.

My favourite teacher at St James's is Big Bill Campbell, especially for English because he reads us books about Tom Sawyer and Huckleberry Finn or Bunter the Fat Owl of the Remove and Harry Wharton and his pals. He's a tall baldy man with a pointy ginger beard and a great voice, because he sometimes reads stories on the radio. I can believe it because when he reads us stories in the class he imitates all the different voices and he makes great faces as well.

I'll give you a little composition, he says to us one day. Just for fun, see how you get on.

He reads out the first paragraph of a story and we have to finish the rest in one page. It's a story about a hunter getting lost in the forest and when his companions go looking for him all they find is this big footprint in the dirt, far too big to be a man's . . .

In my story they wander about terrified that some kind of monster is stalking them and one of them nearly dies of heart failure when a rifleshot rings out not far from them. But when they follow the sound they find the first hunter sitting as cool as a cucumber on the carcase of a huge grizzly bear he's just shot, with his rifle across his knees and a Player's in his mouth. And then he tells them the story of his adventures . . .

I take a lot of trouble with my story because it's for Big Bill, and I try my hardest to make it like the adventure stories I read in the *Hotspur* and the *Wizard*. I even give it a title, A Hairsbreadth Escape, I'm that proud of it.

But that's nothing to how I feel when Big Bill gives us our marks. At first it looks as if the highest mark is eight and a half out of ten to Jim McColl, and McColl is dead chuffed because that's very high, even better than Rosemary McKim. But Big Bill is keeping my story to the end, he says, because he wants to read it out to the whole class. And that's what he does, and I sit there blushing all through it, dead embarrassed though of course I'm pleased as well. But the next thing he says makes this the happiest day of my life.

I'm going to give you top marks for that John, he says. Ten out of ten, a mark I hardly ever give. In fact I've only given it once before, a long time ago, to a boy in my class, and that boy is now training to be a journalist on the *Daily Telegraph* in London.

I hardly hear a word he says after that, or McColl either, when he comes up to shake hands and say Put it there, pal. That's to show he's a good sport and doesn't mind coming second to somebody like me who's going to be famous one day. Because in my mind I'm already the ace reporter on a big London paper lounging with my feet on the desk, soft hat pushed back on my head and the phone wedged under my chin. My pencil is poised over my notebook. *Boyle of the* Telegraph *here*, I drawl, *Just give me the facts.* Then I'm bent over an old iron typewriter with my tie loose and my collar open, hammering out my latest big crime story at the speed of a machine gun. There's a Player's stuck in the corner of my mouth, and my eyes are screwed up to see through the smoke. A cynical grin plays about my lips.

It's an odd feeling, serving Mass on Sunday. Before Mass starts the altarboy has to go out onto the dark altar and light all the candles. You use a long pole with a burning taper on the end and a wee brass cone next to it; that's for putting the flame out again after Mass. You go out there in your black soutane and sandshoes and white surplice and even if there's not many people in church you have to look holy because you're on the altar. The Tabernacle is where the Blessed Host is: you genuflect every time you cross in front of it. The candles are on high brass stands at the back of the altar and sometimes the wick on one of them gets stuck in the hardened candlegrease and won't light and you stand there mortified and sweating because you know people are watching you. You can hear them coming in behind you all the time and shuffling along the pews and kneeling down waiting for Mass to start and because the altar is still dark you know you're all there is for them to look at. The pole gets heavy when you hold it up for a long time and then the end starts wobbling so it's even harder to guide the wee flame onto the wick. You see the flame wavering and missing the candle and you know they can all see it as well. It's even worse when there's two of you and Foley or McDowall has finished his side already, no bother, and has to stand waiting for you at the bottom of the steps. You keep your back turned so nobody can see the panic on your face, or the relief when the candle lights at last. Then you put your holy face back on and turn and come back down the steps. You keep your eyes down that holy way so you don't look at the people but you feel them looking at you. You feel it on your face. It's a funny feeling, a good feeling, feart and proud at the same time. You try to move slow and steady as if to say, No bother, everything is how it should be. When you reach the other altarboy you turn and genuflect to the Tabernacle, the two of you in perfect time, then slow and solemn, like in a procession, you walk back to the vestry.

I hate going to Paisley Baths. I hate the hospital smell mixed in with the smell of drains and pee and sweaty feet in the showers. The hospital smell comes off the water. It's a funny greenish colour and freezing cold. I hate the cold slippy feel of the stone floor around the pool and the way the other boys run mad around it screaming and pushing and jumping in making big splashes. The shouts and the splashes echo twice as loud because of the stone floors and the green tiles and the high skylights. The good swimmers are always pushing or dragging each other in, but I can't swim at all so the only safe place for me is in the water at the shallow end holding on to the side.

Our class is at Paisley Baths because we're getting swimming lessons from a teacher, Mr Gregg, who used to swim for the West of Scotland. He's in the water at the shallow end waiting for us to jump in, one after the other. Don't worry boys, he says, I'll catch you if you fall. It's all right for the other boys, they jump in all the time but I'm terrified. I can jump off a high dyke onto the ground easy enough but this is different; the water pushes up under your feet so you don't land right and you can twist your ankle or go under and choke. But I can't explain this to Mr Gregg, he's waiting there saying, Come along boy, nothing to be afraid of, there's nothing to it, I'm here to catch you. At last I have to jump but I'm that feart it's more like a fall with my arms stretched out because I'm desperate in case I go under. But still I miss his hand and stumble forward and get green water in my mouth and eyes and up my nose before he grabs me and I come up spluttering and gasping. And he's laughing, There now, that wasn't so bad, was it? and the other boys are laughing as well. And I'm more feart than ever and dead embarrassed because I know I'm the worst in the class at this and now everybody else will know.

After a while the lesson part is finished and we're supposed to practise on our own. I just hide at the shallow end holding onto the side until Mr Gregg blows the whistle and says, Right boys, everybody out in two minutes. A lot of boys scramble out to try and be first in the showers so for a while the water's nice and calm, there's nobody near me except Charlie Miller who's doing breadths underwater.

Charlie's a great swimmer.

'S dead easy, he's always telling me. Nuthin' tae it.

I move gingerly out from the side and crouch down in the water and try the breast stroke. I even risk taking my feet off the bottom and doing a frog-kick because I know it's safe, I can put my feet back down. I'm doing stroke, kick, feet down, stroke, kick, feet down and moving slowly towards the deep end but it's OK, my head is still well out of the water when I stand up. Then I think, Time to get out, time for a last stroke, kick and I'm putting my feet down when somebody grabs my ankles from behind and jerks them up and my face goes under. I gasp for air and gulp water. Then I come up threshing my arms to try and get my balance and I can feel my big toe stubbing on the bottom but I fall forward again and choke on more water. When I come up somebody's laughing, it sounds like Charlie standing somewhere to the side shouting, Ye see? Whit'd I tell ye? Ye're swimmin'! And down I go again, into the cloudy green silence with the noise of my ears gurgling inside my head and my heart bursting, then back up to the loud echoey glare of the baths. In a panic I try and breathe and shout Help! but I only choke again on green water and I'm back under in the dead silence clawing for something to hold onto but there's nothing and I think, Ah'm droonin', Ah'm gonnae die, and I try to howl but I can't.

There's a tremendous splash near me and there's something in the water: my hand lands on a big white body. I clutch at it with all the strength I've got left and dig my fingers in and hang on. A'right, ye're a'right! Jeez! Keep the heid! somebody shouts and I can feel his arms going round my chest and grabbing me, steadying me, pulling me back, back. Then I feel the tiles under my feet and I'm standing up in the water coughing and choking and hanging onto somebody and I won't let go. I can't see who it is because my eyes are stinging and streaming.

Ye're a'right, he says. Ye can let go noo, ye can let go! Ye're a'right, don't worry.

It's big Cullen, a big fat boy from a higher class, a great swimmer. Sometimes we call him Billy Bunter and laugh at him behind his back because he wears these wee round specs. His eyes look funny without them. There's a big red scratch right down the front of his chest and he's bleeding into the water.

Later on, when we're out of the pool and Mr Gregg has examined me, shaking his head and tut-tutting, Why didn't you get out of the pool when you were

142

told, boy? I point at the red marks on big Cullen's chest and ask, Whit happened to you?

He looks down and says, That wiz you. When you grabbed oantae me. But it's a'right, ye couldnae help it.

In the bus going back to school I find bits of his skin under my nails.

We're playing football at St James's one day when the ball gets burst. It's a rubber ball about half-way between a tennis ball and a fullsize cudger and when big McKean toes it up the park to clear it it bursts. We try and keep playing for a while but there's a big slit in the ball and it starts to go all wobbly and floppy so it's no use, we have to give up. I'm on Big Owen's side and we're cheesed off because we were winning 3–1 with five minutes to go and now Duignan's side are all shouting It's a draw! The gemme's a bogey! I pick up what's left of the ball and start footering about with it. The slit in it is that big I can tear it in half and I'm left with two bits that look like daft rubber swimming caps and I stick one on my head for a laugh. Then I creep up behind Big Owen where he's sitting on the steps and stick the other one on his head. I don't know what comes over me; I'm happy because we were winning, I suppose, and I wasn't playing too bad.

Fancy gaun fur a swim, eh? I say to Big Owen. Might as well, eh? We've goat the bunnets!

Some of the boys laugh but Big Owen's in a bad mood about the game. He swipes the rubber off his head and slings it at me.

Watch it, Boyle, he says, you're askin' fur it, and for a minute I'm worried, because Big Owen's one of the best fighters in the school. The other boys are standing

143

there watching. Probably hoping he's going to give me a hammering.

But he gets a better idea. You can see him thinking it. He looks around till he sees Wee Joe Moore, then nods towards me.

Right, Joe, he says. Get 'um!

The other boys start laughing and jeering because they think Big Owen's just having a laugh. But the truth is I've always been feart of Wee Joe Moore: there's something scary about him. He comes from this housing scheme near St James's called Shortroods: they're dead rough there, even the weans. Whenever Wee Joe gets into a fight he goes mad, kicking and scratching and biting. He never fights fair, never even thinks about it, you can tell. Once he starts fighting, he just doesn't care. You only have to look at him, his dead eyes and his raggy clothes, and you know he's got nothing to lose. Whatever it is about him, it puts the fear of God into me.

Big Owen must know that. I don't know how, but he knows.

I can't let the boys see how feart I am so I start acting really terrified, putting it on a bit, as if I'm just doing it for a laugh.

Oh aye, I say, That'll be right. Ohmammydaddy, help me Ah'm dead scairt!

They're all laughing now, joining in the game. At least that's what they think.

Aye, that's it, Joe!

Go'n get 'um!

Seize 'um!

But when Wee Joe starts walking towards me I know he's in dead earnest. So I back away and then break into a run across the playground, still clowning and

144

shouting, Help, help, murder polis, get the polis, that man's gonnae murder me!

And Wee Joe just keeps coming after me, like a bloodhound, as if he can scent how feart I really am.

We get all the way across the playground with me still dodging and acting the clown and Wee Joe never far behind me, till we come to the wall on the other side. I've got to turn and face him, there's nowhere else to go. I stand there with my back to the wall and I'm still laughing away like a madman but inside I'm dying with fear.

He's stopped about two or three steps away from me, breathing hard. Some of the boys have followed us across the playground and they gather round us, closing us in. They're still laughing and jeering, waiting to see what happens. I don't even know who's there or what they're saying, it's all a blur.

Go fur 'im Joe! Ye've goat 'um coarnered!

Over to the side somewhere, there's a bunch of lassies giggling. They're just a blur as well, but then I see one of them flicking her black hair a way I would know anywhere, and I hear May Kane's voice.

Oh look, she says. It's a fight.

Sounding huffy and bored, as if to say, So what?

How can she say that? She's got no idea what's going on.

Any minute now I'll be shamed for ever. I'll never be able to face her or Big Owen or Foley or McColl again. I'm going to have to fight Joe Moore and it might as well be Joe Louis for all the chance I've got.

I just stand there. I don't know what to do.

Then the bell goes, and I realize two things: I can't let myself be shamed in front of May Kane, and any minute now there'll be teachers in the playground.

Even if Wee Joe Moore duffs me up they're bound to stop it before he can do too much damage.

I've got to take him on. I've got nothing to lose.

I give him a hard stare as if to say, Right, that's enough o' this cairry-oan. Trying to act like Johnny Mack Brown.

Right, Moore, I say to him. You've asked fur it.

And I charge.

The next thing I know, Wee Joe's flat on his back and I'm kneeling on his shoulders with my hands round his neck strangling him. I can hardly believe how easy it was to knock him over and keep him down. He's much lighter than me. I should know that from playing football: any time he tackles me he just bounces off me. But that's football; there's rules in football. It's different in a fight.

D'ye gi'e in? I shout at him.

Ah'll fight ye efter school, he's trying to say. It comes out all choked and wheezy because I'm strangling him. But I don't want to fight him after school. No chance. I'd never make it through the afternoon. This is the only chance I've got.

Ya wee coward, I shout at him. If ye want tae fight, ye'll fight me noo!

I'm just saying that. I don't want to fight him now or anytime. But I start banging his head off the ground to show I'm in earnest.

Awright, awright! he says, Ah gi'e in!

I give his head one last thump just to make sure then I get off him and let him up. And that's it finished. I can hardly believe it. The teachers are out now on the big steps on the other side and we all have to get back over there and line up.

Wee Joe's ahead of us, on his own, hurrying to get

away. He looks that skinny and pathetic I can hardly believe how feart I was. I walk gallous and easy among the boys though I'm giddy with excitement. Then the bunch of lassies hurry past us whispering and because I know May Kane's there I hold my head high like Caratacus, aloof and proud, not bothered at all.

I see her black hair tossing as she goes past.

That's a sin, she says, so it is. A big lump like that fightin' a puir wee boay!

I'm flattened. It's like a punch on the nose, only worse. But then Big Owen falls in beside me. Big smile.

Battler Boyle, eh? he says, and he gives me a pally punch on the arm, up on the muscle, just hard enough to hurt me.

As if to say, Ye're lucky it wisnae me ye wur fightin'.

But I'm not bothered, because all I can think about is the light in his eyes when he called me Battler Boyle.

Of course I know I'm not really a battler, not compared to born battlers like Big Owen or Wee Joe Moore. To tell the truth, in my heart I sometimes feel like a bit of a sissy. But now I know I'm bigger than most boys my age and I can act tough if I'm pushed to it, and that'll have to do.

It's funny how the tenements are different at night, when the street's deserted and dark except for wee cones of brightness under the lampposts and the odd wafer of light at a window where there's somebody still up and it's that dead quiet you can hear the rumble and whine of a late tram going past, miles away up the town. Sometimes I'm playing down at the dead end of Galloway Street and the other weans have all gone in because it's getting late but I've lost track of time so I'm

147

the only one still out. I do that sometimes and get a row from my mammy, though it's glad of it she should be, or so you'd think, with the houseful of weans we've got now, especially since she came back from the hospital with another baby, wee Bernard. But it seems she's always moaning about me these days.

The way that fella does be dreaming and doting half the time, I hear her saying one day to Auntie Margaret, I declare to God, he's like a man in a trance.

It's creepy walking back up Galloway Street on your own in the dark, when the only noise is your footsteps and the echoes they make on the other side of the street, especially when you're wearing leather soles with the wee steel tips my daddy always puts on the heels to make them last longer. The echo sounds like somebody keeping time with you, an invisible man marching in step along the opposite pavement, keeping you company.

Sometimes I whistle a wee tune to cheer myself up, like 'Marie's Weddin'' or 'Roamin' in the Gloamin'', and I march along in time to it, heel for heel and toe for toe, remembering the words in my head.

Roamin' in the gloamin', be the bonny banks o' Clyde
Roamin' in the gloamin', wi' a lassie by my side

When you go past a close the echo changes: you hear a double echo that's even louder out the back of the close on the other side, as if there's somebody else pounding along through the backdoors over there, some giant in seven league boots, making giant strides, a close at a time.

FEE! FI! FO! FUM!

And all you can do is whistle louder.

WHEN THE SUN GOES DOWN TO REST, THAT'S THE TIME
    THAT I LOVE BEST,
ROAMIN' SOFTLY ROAMIN' IN THE GLOAMIN'!

I like to imagine that the invisible man marching in
step with me on the other pavement is my Guardian
Angel, just making sure I'm all right. But I get worried
about the giant galumphing through the backdoors. I try
to kid myself on it's another Guardian Angel, maybe the
one that looks after mine. But in my heart I know it
could be some evil spirit, maybe even the Devil himself,
and that's a terrifying thought. But whatever it is, I keep
telling myself, I've got nothing to be feart about, nothing
at all; isn't my Guardian Angel walking along beside
me, alert to the danger, shielding me from harm?

1951

Ah'm gonnae try it staunin' on the seat, Wullie says.

It's Sunday afternoon and it's raining and me and
Wullie Deveney are over at the swings at Brown's
Place.

There's nobody else about. It's not raining too bad,
just spitting. But it's been pouring all day and the sky
is black and grey. The seats are waterlogged, the
wood's all heavy and soggy. When you sit on it your
trousers get soaked and stick to your bum.

But standing up's no use either because the wood's
that heavy it's dead hard to get the swing to go up high
and our legs get tired.

D'ye no think we should chuck it?

I say that but I know we'll stick it because we're the
only ones there. Usually the swings are crowded with

149

scruffy weans from Brown's Place shouting and shoving and you have to wait ages for your turn.

We invent a new game. You stand at one side of the frame and pull the chains on one swing back then let the seat go so it swings across and bangs into the pole on the other side. When you see where it hits, one of you has to grip the pole at that place. Then you say Ready and the other one launches the swing. It's a dare. You have to keep your hand on the pole till the last minute, then pull it away. The one that keeps his hand there the longest is the winner.

The seat's dead heavy because of the rain and when it bangs into the iron pole it makes a deep *boing!* noise and the whole frame shudders. All the chains jangle and the seats bounce up and down. It's great.

We play this game for a long time even though it's started getting dark. We keep arguing about who was last to take his hand away. Wullie says he's winning 9–7 and I say it's a draw eight each.

So we say we'll play one more to decide who's the winner. I'm determined to keep my hand on the pole till the last split second. I watch Wullie dragging the chains towards him and getting the seat ready, aiming at my hand. Now it's dark he's sighting along the edge of it like a rifle. I'm jealous I never thought of that. If I do it next time he'll say I'm just copying him. So I grip the pole really hard instead and hiss my breath back through my teeth to show I'm in earnest, like a tough guy in the gangster comics.

OK, Palooka, I say, this is the showdown!

At least that's what I mean to say but I never get to the end because Wullie thinks OK Palooka means Ready and he fires the seat at me dead fast and it squashes my hand against the pole.

The shock is that bad it knocks the breath out of me.
The sky birls.

I'm going to faint.

I flop down on my hunkers holding my broken hand and howling. The pain is terrible. I'm feart I'm going to die.

Ohmammydaddy   Ohmammydaddy   Ohmammydaddy

It's me saying that. I keep saying it. I can't stop greetin'.

What stops me is that Wullie starts greetin' himself. He's kneeling beside me shouting Ah'm sorry Johnny, Ah'm sorry, Ah didnae mean it, honest. He's feart if I tell my mammy his daddy will half kill him with the belt. If they think he broke my hand on purpose he might even get sent to Borstal.

Ah didnae mean it, Johnny, he keeps saying. Cross ma heart.

He sounds that feart I feel sorry for him.

It's OK Wullie, I whisper back. It's OK, Ah'll no' tell, honest.

We get up and look at my hand. It's all red and it's throbbing like mad but it doesn't look too bad except for one finger. My first finger is swelled up and the nail is turning black and blue. It's still dead sore but it's going numb now and I can feel my breath coming back.

Jist as well it's ma left haun, eh? I say. So Ah'll still be able tae write 'n that.

I'm trying to sound casual and tough because he saw me greetin'.

Oh hey so ye wull!

He's dead relieved. If I can go to school tomorrow I might not have to tell anybody what happened.

On the way back over to Galloway Street I practise

keeping my sore hand in my trouser pocket. I try to make a fist but the finger is stiff, I can't bend it.

In the close Wullie stops me at the bottom of the stairs.

Promise ye'll no' tell?

Cross ma heart.

Scout's honour?

Scout's honour.

We're not in the scouts but we always say that.

Shake?

We shake hands and go up the stairs.

When I get in my mammy asks me where I've been.

Ower at the swings wi' Wullie Deveney.

Lord above, in this weather? Ye're mad, the pair o' ye.

But that's all she says. My Auntie Mary her sister from Achill is staying with us and the two of them are sitting by the fire blethering about Home.

It's going to be OK.

I wake up in the night greetin' with my sore finger throbbing and pounding under the blankets and the pain worse than ever. I must've been greetin' in my sleep, because my mammy's standing over me wondering what's wrong.

I have to tell her.

It wis an accident Mammy, honest. Wullie jumped aff the swing when it was still goin' and it swung back and banged intae ma haun.

She looks suspicious but I think she believes me. She makes me take a tablespoon of medicine for the pain, then I lie there with my hands on my chest and my finger sticking up in the air because that'll keep the blood out of it, she says, and it won't be so sore.

Splash.

Splash.

I'm on a ship out at sea. I think it's the same ship my Uncle Pat's on but I don't know where he is. I hear the waves washing against the side and feel the bed swaying under me. Or is it a hammock? I feel a bit dizzy but not sick.

I've been sleeping. The sound of the waves is what's waking me up.

Splash, then nothing.

Splash, then nothing.

Splash, then somebody splutters and coughs.

I'm not on a ship at all. I'm lying in my bed in the big room at home and my Auntie Mary's washing her face in a basin of water on the chest of drawers by the window.

She's bent over the basin with her back to me. She doesn't know I'm watching her. She's got her hair done up in a turban with a towel and she's only wearing a cream slip with a lacy top. I can see the straps all squeegee on her bare shoulders. Her arms are dead white with dark hair under the oxters.

She's the only one of my aunties that's not married and I don't know if I'm supposed to be looking so I shut my eyes. But I'm still keeking through the slits.

I'm still sleepy.

Splash.

Splash.

I hear the wash of the waves again and see my Uncle Pat up at the prow of the ship. He's got his Player's

153

Please beard and his bus driver's uniform and cap and he's pointing and shouting back to me. His voice is faint and fading away.

Land ahoy, he shouts. Land ahoh-oy!

I'm in Winchburgh with my Auntie Mary to visit the Mullens. She wants to see her sister Bridget and her family before she goes back to Ireland and my mammy's sent me with her because it's a long bus journey to the other side of Scotland and Mary's never been there before.

When we get off the bus from Broxburn two raggedy-looking weans come up to us. I nearly don't recognize them at first, then I see it's my cousins, Young Peter and Packy, his wee brother. Billy's the one that's my age but he's not with them. My auntie Mary's never seen the Mullens before and she grips me tight by the hand as if they were beggars or something and tries to march us right past them. It's a bit embarrassing.

It's a' right, Auntie Mary, I tell her. It's only Peter and Packy Mullen. They're my cousins. Auntie Bridget's boys.

They're not, are they? says Auntie Mary. Are ye sure? Begod, they're wildlookin' altogether. Tinkers, more like it, by the looks o' them.

She's in dead earnest, but I just laugh and kid on it's only a joke, and Peter and Packy don't seem to be bothered, they just keep dodging and jookin' around us and laughing and asking questions. When I ask about Billy they say he didn't want to come. I can imagine that; he's dead moody sometimes.

It's great visiting Auntie Bridget's house in Winchburgh. It's not like Galloway Street because here it's all wee houses side by side in rows – the *raws* they call them – and so there's no stairs and no closes and every house has its Own Door. That's my mammy's dream, to have her Own Door. In fact these houses have two Own Doors, the front and the back. In Winchburgh they always go in the back door: through the gate and the wee garden and into the scullery. Then you go up a step and you're in the main kitchen, where Uncle Peter sits in his chair by the hob reading his paper and Auntie Bridget stands at the table pouring out this strong black tea she always makes and cursing the boys.

Ye're wild altogether, so ye are, ye'll drive me to the grave yet, may the Almighty God curse an' damn ye to Hell. Aye, let the Devil look after ye, an' see how ye like that, an' let ye burn and fry down there, it's all ye deserve, for ye're a bad lot, ye're evil, so ye are, amathons and latchykos the lot o' ye.

My mammy curses sometimes and I don't like it, but my Auntie Bridget's curses are much worse, she stands there effing and blinding and saying swearwords my mammy would never say. She keeps on cursing even when she's putting milk and sugar in our tea or cutting bread and cheese for our pieces. She calls the boys every name under the sun, but the worst is when she calls down curses on their heads. That's what makes me really feart because it's worse than swearing, she's condemning her own weans to Hell and damnation.

The boys never seem that bothered, they just laugh and make daft faces at me behind her back. Or so they think. Sometimes she'll catch them at it and she'll hit one of them an almighty skelp on the back of the head. Then it's:

Aw Maw! It wisnae me! It wiz him!

That's Young Peter, pointing at Billy or Packy. Or one of them pointing at him. Wee Tommy's only a baby, the Bairn they call him; he's too wee to get into trouble yet.

And through all this Uncle Peter just sits there dead quiet, reading his paper by the hob. Sometimes I'll see him lowering the paper and giving her a hard look over the top of it, but without saying anything. Then when she keeps going and her language gets even worse, he lets his hands drop into his lap so the paper makes a loud crumpling noise and he says:

That's enough, wummin! Mind yer tongue!

He doesn't shout or anything, but you can see from his face he's in dead earnest. He's a tall skinny man, with a pale face and a long jaw and he hardly ever says a word. But when he does, you listen. My Auntie Bridget keeps on moaning for a while but it's not so bad now, you can see she's winding down, and eventually she stops.

My Uncle Peter's my favourite of the Mullens, because he's the quiet one. He hardly ever takes a drink, even though he never took the Pledge like Barney Molloy. He walks with a stoop because of his bad back and he moves about the house slow and steady. He works at the pit, though he's only fit for light work nowadays. But I can remember how he used to come in with his face grey with shaledust so his eyes and teeth were the only white you saw. How he'd strip to the waist and wash his face and his thin grey body in the wee scullery by the door before he came into the house.

There's something holy about my Uncle Peter, although he never talks about it and he never tries to force anybody else to be holy. He'll sit there reading by the fire late at night when we're all talking round the table. Then he looks up at the clock, folds his paper, gets up, turns round and goes down slowly on his knees with his elbows on the chair and his face in his hands and starts saying his prayers under his breath. The first time I see him doing this I'm dead embarrassed and I look at Billy and Young Peter but they only shrug and look awkward and I realize this is something their father does every night.

Faither. That's what they call him.

And though I pretend not to look I can't help watching him, his long face pale and serious behind his fingers and his lips moving silently, like Father Murphy praying before morning Mass. But Father Murphy's a priest, that's his job, and it's one thing to be holy in a sacred place like the vestry; it's another thing to be like Uncle Peter, kneeling down every night to say his prayers in front of rowdy weans that are always arguing and fighting and a wife ranting and cursing at them like the Queen of the Gypsies. It seems to me it takes a brave man to do that, and I think that's what I like best of all about my Uncle Peter.

Winchburgh's a funny place, it's not like Paisley at all. There's a big hill at the back of the town they call the bing. But it's not a real hill, Auntie Bridget's always warning us, it's only a tip made with shale from the pit, and we're not to go near it, she says, because it's dangerous, it could collapse any minute and ye'd be buried in the muck and then where would ye be? But Billy and Peter and Packy play there sometimes and I have to go with them or they'd call me a coward.

One time me and Billy fall out because he's in one of his moods. But then he kids on everything's OK and

157

says we'll play hide and seek and I can be het. And even though it's getting dark I say all right, glad he's not in a huff any more. So I sit there near the top of the bing with my eyes shut and count up to twenty. Then I start looking for them. They're not in the usual places, behind the bushes or in the wee hollows you get in the side of the bing. I go right round the other side and there's still no sign of them. Then I start shouting their names because there's no sign of anybody else either and I'm getting feart up there all on my own. Billy's sneaked away with his wee brothers and left me. It's getting cold now as well as dark and I'm dead worried because I'm not sure how to get back to their house even in the daytime. So I scramble back down the slope as fast as I can.

By the time I get down it's dark all about me. I can see lights in the houses in the distance but no street-lights and I don't know where I am. Then I think I can make out the dark hump of the school building in its flat playground and I walk over that way because it's near where the Mullens' house is. I'm walking through the dark raws at the edge of the village but I don't know these houses and there's nobody I can ask. And all at once a dark shape like a tall man comes round the far corner of the raws in front of me and I get the fright of my life, because it's just a long black shadow with no face, except for one huge eye burning in its forehead, so bright it blinds me to look at it. It's like the ogre we've read about in fairytales and legend, a monster with one Cyclops eye in the middle of its head and I'm that feart I can hardly move, I just stand there as it comes towards me, too feart even to run.

And then, when it's only about six yards from me, the monster stoops to open a gate and disappears into one of the houses in front of me. I'm still standing there wondering if I saw what I think I saw when I hear footsteps behind me and the low murmur of men's voices. Thank God for that, I'm thinking, weak with relief, and I turn round to see who it is.

And this time I nearly pass out. Because it's a whole gang of the same giants, five or six of them, coming at me out of the dark with the single eyes burning in their heads and wee dots of light where their mouths should be. I can't move, there's nowhere to hide, they're nearly on top of me, I'm a goner for sure . . . and then they've trudged past me and it's only a gang of black-faced miners coming off their shift with the lamps in their helmets shining and wee fag-ends glowing in their mouths.

Watchers of the Night.

Ye a' right, son? one of them says as he goes past. Ye better be gettin' awa' hame noo, it's gettin' daurk.

Even though she's kindhearted and always nice to me, I'm a bit feart of my Auntie Bridget and the lash of her tongue, she looks that fierce when she's angry: she's got a strong Gypsy face and black hair and her eyes glitter. But when she's in a good mood she's got a beautiful smile. She's my mammy's big sister and you can see the resemblance to her and Auntie Mary and Auntie Annie. I always think my mammy's the best-looking sister, except when Auntie Bridget smiles; then her eyes shine and her teeth flash and her strong face softens and you've got to admit she's the beauty.

But that's not the face we see the night I turn up at Winchburgh with Auntie Mary.

All the time Bridget is setting the table with the good tablecloth and putting out the plates of scones and

159

biscuits she's asking me about my mammy and daddy and the rest of the family in Paisley. She hardly says a word to Mary, even though she's sitting there beside me. It's a bit odd because they haven't seen each other for years and you'd think they would have a lot of news about Home to catch up on. And maybe Mary thinks the same because after a while she says something about how nice the tea is, and the scones, and what a lovely tablecloth. And Bridget stops what she's doing and stares at her across the table.

Oh, she says. Are we good enough for ye, is that it?

I can see Mary doesn't know what she means. Bridget just stands there looking at her. She's not that angry looking; she's even smiling a wee bit. But it's not her real smile, far from it.

By God ye've changed yer tune, says Auntie Bridget. It's a wonder ye wouldn't have the gumption to say it to our faces.

Arra what are ye talkin' about for the love o' God? says Mary. She's trying to make a joke of it. She turns to me and giggles, but it comes out forced and false.

Do *you* know what she's talking about? she says.

Leave the child alone, says Auntie Bridget. It's nothing to do with him. He's not the one calling us tinkers.

Mary's still trying to smile but she looks as if she's been slapped. Her mouth falls open and her whole face flushes. She starts to deny she said any such thing but Bridget cuts her off.

Don't go making yerself a liar and a coward, says Bridget. Isn't it bad enough that ye have a snake's tongue on you? Coming here with your airs and graces, calling us tinkers. Miss Hoity toity, high and mighty, and herself working down in England in some dirty

160

oul' factory. Lady Muck is more like it. Do ye ever look at yerself, I wonder. Or listen to yerself? By God it would do ye good, I'm telling ye . . .

She says a lot more than this and there's nothing any of us can do except sit there and listen, even Mary though you can see she's mortified. And the funny thing is, not once does Bridget raise her voice or her hand, the way she does with the boys, and not once does she curse or swear, and yet I've never been more feart of her than that night, my Auntie Mary's first night in Winchburgh.

I'm going to Ireland!

My mammy asks me about it the day Doctor Pat comes to lance my sore finger and put a new bandage on it. My Auntie Mary's going back Home, she says, and how would I like to go back to Ireland with her for a holiday? It'll mean sailing across the Irish Sea and maybe going to school for a wee while in Achill. She says this as though she's not too sure about it herself, and at first I'm worried she might be trying to get rid of me altogether. But it doesn't last. I've never been on a big ship before, just wee boats at Rothesay and Dunoon, and though I'm a bit feart it might sink I keep that to myself.

Aye, definitely, I tell her. Ah'd love tae go!

I think maybe she tells me about Ireland to cheer me up before the doctor comes because she knows what he's going to do to me and I don't.

What he does is rip off my bad nail and throw it in the fire.

It's the worst pain I've ever felt in my life. It's worse because I'm not expecting the shock, not really. Doctor Pat looks at my finger which is still swollen up all

161

yellow and purply with the nail nearly black and hanging off.

I'm afraid that's going to have to come off, he says.

I nearly panic because I think he means my finger and he laughs, No, no, you can keep your finger, John, it's just the nail, that nail'll have to go. We're standing there by the fire and he's that calm and friendly I think he means, someday, in the hospital maybe. Not here, not now. Even when he gets these wee pliers out and starts moving my nail up and down it hardly hurts me and I think he's just checking it, maybe, getting a bit of practice for the operation.

And then the sudden wrench and the stab of sheer agony, and the sizzle my nail makes when he flicks it into the fire. A wee purple flame pops and flares.

I sook my breath in hard through my teeth but I have to stop myself greetin' because my mammy and Auntie Mary are there watching. And Doctor Pat is busy putting stuff on my finger, gauze and bandages, and wrapping it tight so I've got another pain to think about now, though it's not half as bad as the first one.

When he's left my Auntie Mary comes over to me, peering into my face.

Are ye not cryin'?

Naw. Ah'm a' right.

I'm not, but what else am I supposed to say?

Begod, she says to my mammy, he's a soldier, isn't he?

They start talking to me about the journey to Ireland, how I'll have to get permission from my teachers at St James's, and the Mother Superior, and what clothes I'll need to take, and after a few minutes I can hardly feel my finger throbbing in the new bandage, I'm that excited to be going on holiday and sailing the seas like

162

my Uncle Pat. I'm not too sure about my Auntie Mary, mind, she has funny ways about her sometimes, so I don't know how much of a holiday it'll be, but I know I can hardly wait to see this place in Ireland my mammy's always talking about, this place she still calls Home.

It's pandemonium getting the night boat to Ireland at the docks in Glasgow. I'm down there with my mammy and Auntie Mary holding me tight by the hand because the crowds are as bad as Love Street on a Saturday, only worse. It's worse because it's getting dark and there's thousands of men and women and old grannies and greetin' weans and everybody shouting and bawling and shoving. And they've all got big bags with them and hard suitcases that keep banging into me though that's not what bothers me, not really; what I can't get over is the size of the ship we're going on. I can see it up there against the dock and it's like a giant tenement with all the lights on; it seems impossible that it could float and not sink. There's big wooden gangways with ropes for rails that go out over the black water and in through big open doors in the side of the ship where I can make out dim lights and the silhouettes of the sailors waiting on board to help the passengers. And jostling up this gangway feels like jostling up the wide steps at Love Street on Saturdays, only worse again because of the noise and the riversmell and our footsteps drumming on the bare boards swaying over the deep drop below and you know if you fall you're doomed to drown in the black water or get crushed to death against the dock.

I don't remember when we get separated from my mammy but the next thing I know I'm squeezed up against the rails in the crowd at the side of the ship with my Auntie Mary behind me and I can barely make out my mammy among the dim figures waving on the dock down below; it's like looking down into Galloway Street from our kitchen window. We stand there waving and waving till the boat shudders and the water churns and a foghorn goes off that makes my heart jump and my skin go shivery then the deck is moving under my feet and the dock with my mammy on it is moving as well, heavy and slow, sliding away past the side of the ship till it disappears in the dark. And I'm thinking I'm like Poor Pat now, her longlost brother who sailed away to sea and was never heard of again from that day to this and I wonder if she's thinking the same.

My Auntie Mary makes me swallow a seasick tablet before I go to sleep. But in the night I dream that me and Poor Pat are the only survivors on a ship lashed by giant waves in a terrible seastorm and when I wake up feart and sick and trying to vomit, all that comes up is the tablet she gave me.

164

Home

In Galloway Street I used to dream of a quiet place where I could go and get peace from people arguing and weans greetin' but here in Achill there's hardly anybody at all. It's a lovely place but dead lonely. There's wee white cottages spread out on the mountain that slopes down to the sea but they're miles apart: you can see the neighbours, just about, but you can't talk to them, you have to shout or maybe just wave.

Auntie Mary's cottage is high up on the slope; in fact there's no other houses there only the Mountain Road as she calls it though to me it just looks like an old dirt track, and beyond that the high hump of the mountain. Inside the house is a dump because nobody's been living there for more than twenty years, and the day we get there and for days after it's teeming with rain so when you look outside all you can see is grey mist, but on days when there's a bit of blue sky you can look down the grassy field sloping past the wee cottage where old Aunt Nancy lives then across the main road to yellow fields of wheat or corn, and all the way down past the flat wet strand to the sea.

*   *   *

Not long after I get to Ireland my Auntie Mary tells me we're going out to the bog for turf to lay in for our fires and my cousin John Fadyen is coming to help us. I'm quite excited, thinking John Fadyen's a boy about my age and maybe we could be pals. So I'm dead disappointed when he turns out to be a grownup man as old as Mary or near enough. He's nice enough, though, a big, slowmoving fellow with dark curly hair and a quiet, smiling way about him.

But I cheer up when I see what he's brought with him, for up there on the mountain road is a brown donkey with two baskets they call creels slung across its back and it turns out John Fadyen is bringing his donkey along with us to carry home the sods of turf and that's why my Auntie Mary asked him to come.

And away we go up the winding mountain road and John Fadyen lets me lead the donkey along by its reins like Johnny Mack Brown with his trusty horse and though I'm a bit nervous of its big bony head and long teeth I'm trying hard not to show it. In fact I'm dying to ask if I can get up on its back even though I know my Auntie Mary would never hear of it. But John Fadyen must guess what I'm thinking because the next thing I know I'm being hoisted up in the air as if I'm no weight at all and planked down on the donkey's bony back with my knees behind the empty creels. And sure enough Mary starts tutting and complaining, For the love o' God, John, will ye take him down from there before he breaks his neck and me supposed to be looking after him? Arra not at all, Mary, says John Fadyen. Sure he's only a gorsoon and what harm will it do him? He'll soon get used to it, and isn't it better now when the creels are empty, or we'd have the poor oul' donkey buggert altogether and him with a full load

166

on the road back? I don't know what he means by gorsoon, but in no time at all he has Mary laughing and joking along with him: Lord above, John, she says, wouldn't it be a grand thing now if we had a camera and could take a snap to send back to Scotland?

I think my Auntie Mary likes John Fadyen.

The bog is a queer place, like no place I've ever seen before, it's like being on the moon. There's miles of brown land with a damp ghosty mist drifting over it and the ground sinks under your feet like swampland and the springy rough heather that grows there scratches your bare legs. And everywhere there's big flat muddy spaces cut out of it in steepsided squares and oblongs and L-shapes like you get in a crossword puzzle, or in the exams at St James's: *Look at the shapes in this sequence and identify the odd one out.* Except here all the shapes are odd. Even the spades John Fadyen and Mary are using are odd, they're L-shaped so the sods come out oblong, like bricks. They come out that soggy and muddylooking I think they'd only put a fire out, never mind light it, but then Mary shows me the wee stacks lying about the bog and they're all dried out, right enough, like horse's dung in Galloway Street when it's been lying a few days, though the turf's got a nicer smell. I wonder why we don't just take the dry stuff and load up the creels with that but John Fadyen only laughs and shakes his head. We'll do that after, all right, he says, As long as 'tis only our own turf we take, for the day every man doesn't shtick to his own bit of bog will be a bad day indeed.

And that's what we do, even though there's only one or two other people on the bog who could see us and they're miles away.

It's hard work digging the turf and we're all puffed out and sweaty at the end of it so John Fadyen builds a wee fire with twigs and dauds of dry turf and Mary makes us tea on it in a big black can with a wire handle looped on the top. It's strong tea, stronger even than Auntie Bridget's in Winchburgh, and it's black with no milk but plenty sugar and though we're drinking out of old tin cans and I can smell the turf off it and taste the blue firesmoke I swear to God it's the best cup of tea I've ever had.

On the way back we meet an old man walking with his donkey and two empty creels. He speaks to John Fadyen, though he keeps looking at me, and I don't understand a word they say because they're talking Irish. But I hear him saying, gorsoon. And John Fadyen says something back to him and I hear the name Sweeney. Then the old man pats me on the head and goes on his way. And Mary explains to me that 'gorsoon' is Irish for 'boy', and the man was just asking who I was. And when John Fadyen told him I was Maggie Sweeney's son from Scotland, the old man said By God he's a Sweeney all right by the cut of him. And I don't know why but it makes me feel proud that I've come back to my mammy's home after all these years and people here think I look like her.

The first day in Achill I ask Auntie Mary where the lavvy is and she looks at me as if I'm mad.

Arra where d'ye think it is? she says. Out there in the byre, where else would it be?

As if that's not bad enough, when I ask if there's any paper out there, she just laughs at me.

Begod but we're choosy, are we? There might be paper there and there might not and if there isn't you can just use a bit of oul' straw like the rest of us.

Squatting out there in the dank, smelly byre I'm trying desperately to keep my balance, to stop myself falling back into my own mess. My knees are sore and I have to keep swatting at the flies buzzing round me and I'm thinking back to the old lavvy on the landing in Galloway Street the way you try to remember a happy dream.

In Ireland I'm surrounded by aunties. There's Auntie Mary, who brought me here for a holiday. There's Aunt Nancy who lives in the cottage down the field from Auntie Mary's and kept an eye on the place while she was away.

Ye're going to a very sad place, *ahashki*, she sighed the day we came to her door for the key. The Lord save us the place is gone to rack and ruin standing empty all these years.

It's true. Auntie Mary's house looks quite nice on the outside, a whitewashed cottage with one door and three windows, with the mountain above it and the sea below, but inside it's a mess. There's no proper furniture only an old dresser and a rickety table in the kitchen, and a bed and dressing table in each of the side rooms and for days after we get there I have to help her clean up all the dust and dirt and fallen plaster. When it's finished, more or less, she takes out this wee framed photo of me that she got from my mammy and stands it on the dresser.

You're the man of the house now, Johnny, she says.

Aunt Nancy is an old woman with no teeth only a black hole where her smile should be and she wears a shawl and a long drab skirt and boots and I think she's too old to be my auntie but Never you mind,

Mary says, Aunt Nancy is what you're to call her and that's all about it.

Aunt Bridgie is the Yank because she's back at home after living for years in Cleveland, Ohio, which is in America.

Cleevelay-end Oh-high-Oh, she says and she smiles at me when she says it. She has false teeth and a nice smile. And she talks about her pocketbook instead of her handbag.

Jest payass me mah packetbeuhk, honey, she'll say to me.

Sometimes the Yank takes me to see Sarah Corrigan who isn't my auntie though I wish she was. Sarah Corrigan is a tall young woman with a beautiful oval face and a lovely smile with teeth that white and perfect you'd swear they were false, except there's a wee chip off one in the front so I know they're not. She lives with her old father in a house up the hill a bit back from the road like Auntie Mary's but much cleaner and nicer with proper furniture, and she's always pleased to see us and puts out plenty of tea in white china cups you can nearly see through and thick slices of soda bread with butter. And she and the Yank have a great natter about the old days in Sraheens before the Yank went away to America.

One time after the tea Sarah Corrigan pats the sofa beside her.

Come over here to me, youngfella, and talk to me for a while.

So over I go and sit beside her and she's asking me all about Scotland and how am I liking it here in Achill. She laughs a lot because I have a cute kind of a way with me, she says, and the way I talk is funny and so are the things I say. And I don't mind her laughing at all because of the way her eyes dance and her teeth shine. Sometimes when she laughs she leans over and gives me a poke in the side and says Ah ye're an awful man altogether and I squirm because it tickles me. Then she starts tickling me in earnest and soon the two of us are giggling away and rolling about on the couch with the Yank sitting there smiling and tutting Ah Sarah ye're as bad as the child, and the old man in his corner shaking his head at this foolishness but puffing away on his pipe, not bothered at all. Then Sarah Corrigan takes me on her knee like a doll or a wee baby she'd be rocking and soon she's tickling me again and hugging me and giving me big wet kisses on the mouth and I'm lying there gasping for breath in her lap with my head in the crook of her arm and my trousers tight on me and my skin all tingly. She's looking down at me with her eyes shining and her laughing mouth is wet and though I'm wriggling to get away it's really so I can feel her warm lap moving under me and burrow my face in her belly that's still quivering from her laughter and all the time I'm praying she'll kiss me again, kiss me again.

Auntie Mary and the Yank are sitting by the turf fire chatting one day when I come running in from outside and they stop when they see me and change to talking Irish. Then Auntie Mary starts asking me questions about Sarah Corrigan and why I'm always asking Aunt Bridgie if she'll take me back there.

Do ye be kissing? she asks me, and she's got this scoffing, scunnered look on her face. I can feel my cheeks burning and I mumble Och it's jist a wee game we play sometimes.

Ah'm sure thurr's no harm in it, Mary, says the Yank and I know she's trying to help. But Auntie Mary only

171

tosses back her head and snorts the way she does when she's angry. And my heart dies in me because I get the feeling I won't be seeing much of Sarah Corrigan again, if I ever do.

Mother Mary Clare, the new head nun at St James's, only let me go to Ireland because my mammy promised her I'd go to school there when the term started up again. So my Auntie Mary takes me down to the school in Achill Sound the first day and leaves me with the nuns.

What are we to do wit' ye at all? says Sister Regis.

She's the Mother Superior. The nuns here wear white habits not black ones and we're to call them Sister not Mother. She asks me questions about our school work in Scotland and I try to tell her but after the long summer holidays I can't remember too much. So she and this other nun just sit there looking at each other and shaking their heads and smiling. Then Sister Regis comes up with the idea of asking me to make up a sum out of my head like the ones I was doing at St James's so they'll know what class to put me in. They give me a jotter and a pencil and leave me to get on with it. I don't like sums and I'm no good at them so I just make up this long multiplication that looks hard but I know I can do without mistakes, hoping they'll put me in a class where the sums'll be easy and I'll be cock of the walk.

But it turns out there's only one class they could put me in anyway. This is the class for boys and girls of ten like me though some are eleven and there's even one boy, Nayliss, who's nearly thirteen and has been in the same class for years. He's a big, slow, glaikitlooking fellow, but he's nice enough with it.

172

I'd say I'm in it for life, Scotty. He smiles at me with big yellow teeth and shrugs his shoulders as if to say, What can ye do?

Scotty is what they call me, and sometimes Jock. Some of the boys are very poorly dressed and come to school in their bare feet. The nuns put me to sit beside a boy called Brian Masterson and I think at first it's because he's got shoes on like me but no, it turns out he lives in the same village, Sraheens.

Shraheens they pronounce it here, with an H. The same way my mammy says it.

Brian becomes my best pal in Ireland. He's good at sums which is just as well because the sums they give us are just as hard as the ones I got at St James's, in fact they're worse because they've got a different way of working things out in Ireland which I can't make head or tail of so the nuns let Brian help me.

Even when I get my sums right they look different from his. He'll look over my shoulder and say, What in the name o' God have ye done there?

My Auntie Mary says Brian Masterson is very old-fashioned because of the queer ways he has of talking. When he's finished his sums he'll watch me still working them out in my foreign Scottish way and say, The Lord bless us and save us, what're ye doin' now? If I manage to get the right answer he lets on to be amazed.

Well now that is uncanny, he'll say, scratching his head. Uncanny is the word for it. That beats the band altogether.

D'ye think could ye make us a sideboard? Auntie Mary says to me one day.

She's always complaining she has no place to keep

173

her flour for baking and packets of oats and tins and things.

Who, me? A sideboard? No, Ah could never do that.

I have to talk a bit posh in Ireland or they'd never understand me.

Ye couldn't? says she. Arra what kind of a man are ye at all?

I feel like telling her I'm not a man, I'm only ten, but I think it might sound childish.

Have ye no gumption, is that it? she says, goading me.

Aye, Ah have! But Ah've got no wood, and no tools!

Haven't I loads of wood out in the oul' shed? And there's a few oul' tools out there, as well. A hammer and a few nails, sure what more do ye want?

And before I know it I'm trying to make a sideboard.

I've never even made so much as a wooden box before so all I can think of is to try and copy our sideboard at home in Galloway Street. But the wood Mary has turns out to be old orange boxes and packing cases and a few old planks in different shapes and sizes, all knotty and twisted with damp. This cheers me up, because surely nobody could make a sideboard out of this pile of old firewood? I know my Auntie Mary will never spend any money to buy decent wood, so I'm beginning to think I might get out of it.

Not a hope.

Arra use it up anyway, Mary says. Won't it be great practice for ye? Let ye try your hand with the old wood. If ye make a job of it, I'll buy some new wood for another try.

It's going from bad to worse. I could end up making two sideboards instead of one. I'm sorry I asked.

So I make a start. Every day after school and at week-ends I'm sawing and hammering away till my hands are blistered and my fingers cut and bruised. I end up with this big oblong box that looks like two empty packing cases nailed together side by side, because that's all it is, plus a few planks nailed on for the top, the front frame and the shelves. But the two sides are different sizes and different woods, and there's faded printing on them that you can still read:

SEAMUS MURPHY, POTATO MERCHANT, BALLINA

PATRICK SWEENEY & SONS, ACHILL SOUND

There's no drawers on it but I've stuck two crude doors on the front with old squares of shoe leather nailed on as hinges. One door is nearly straight, but the other one slumps down to one side no matter what I do to it.

It looks terrible, but Auntie Mary seems pleased enough.

Well done, she says. Begod, aren't ye the champ!

She drags Brian Masterson in to see it one day when we're back from school. I'm mortified but I can't stop her.

There ye are now, she says, waving her hand at it, What d'ye think o' that?

To listen to her you'd think she was showing him a brand new three-piece suite. Brian stands there in the doorway gawping, and for once in his life he's stuck for words.

Isn't it coming along grand? says Mary.

Well, says Brian, It's coming along. I'll say that.

Ah it is, it is surely, says Auntie Mary. All it needs now is a lick o' paint and it'll be as right as rain.

I can see what she means. A coat or two of thick

brown paint might cover up the different colours and the printed words. It might at least look as if it's all the same wood.

But Auntie Mary has no intention of buying paint. She's got an old pot in the shed that has to be used up.

Waste not want not, she says. It's Forest Green, it'll be lovely.

Forest Green is what it says on the rusty old tin, right enough, but it turns out to be a drab khaki that reminds me of an Army tank and no matter how much I stir it it goes on lumpy and streaky, as if the sideboard's in full camouflage. But at last it's finished, or at least I am.

My sideboard squats there for weeks glowering at us from the corner and creaking and swaying every time you touch it, till one by one its drooping doors fall off and at long last Auntie Mary lets me drag it out of the house, back to the shed, back to the firewood it always was at heart.

I'm watching a bluebottle drowning in a barrel. It's an old rainbarrel round the back of Auntie Mary's house and it's always full because it's always raining.

I lean over the barrel some days and look at my reflection in the water. I see a wee boy's dark head and shoulders framed in a big circle and nothing around him but empty grey sky. He looks lost and lonely in there, like an orphan abandoned by his mammy and daddy or marooned like poor Ben Gunn in a faraway land and it makes me feel dead sorry for my reflection.

But this day there's a bluebottle making ripples. At first you'd think it's swimming – as if it landed in the water on purpose. For a dip, like a duck on a pond. Then you can see it's panicking, going in circles, like a wee rowing boat with just the one oar. It's getting slower and slower.

Then it stops.

I slide a leaf under it and lift it out, and lay the leaf on the edge of the barrel.

The bluebottle is soaked. It's just a black blob on the leaf, not moving. I think it's a goner.

I'll leave it there and see.

When we come out of school one day a wee white dog runs up and starts jumping and skipping around us. It's a funnylooking thing, a kind of dirty white all over with droopy ears and tail and Brian Masterson says it's like no class of dog he's seen before on this earth, and by God he's seen some quare specimens. But I feel sorry for it and throw sticks for it to fetch though it just half chases after them in a daft sort of way then comes running back to us with its long tongue hanging out. Ye could be throwing sticks for that dog till Kingdom Come, says Brian, and the divil a stick would he bring back to you for there isn't a drop of sinse in his head.

When we're walking home along the Bog Road the wee dog follows us even though we try to chase it away and Brian says it probably thinks this is just another game like throwing the stick. But I'm thinking to myself it would be great to have a dog, it'll be grand company for Banger the big old sheepdog that lies outside the door at Aunt Nancy's and I tell Brian if it follows me all the way home I'll keep it and call it Speed. And Brian laughs and shakes his head. Ye can call him any name ye like, he says, as long as it's you he follows and not me, for they'd hunt me out of the house if I arrived home with that sorrylookin' craitchur.

177

It's still following me when I run up the field to Aunt Nancy's shouting come on Speed, come on boy, then it runs ahead of me and stops when it sees old Banger at the door and stands there wagging its tail. But Banger gets up growling and runs out and nips it on the leg and Speed runs away yelping and squealing like a mad dog and Banger's barking and Aunt Nancy and the Yank come rushing out to see what all the commotion is and Auntie Mary comes down the path from the cottage above on the hill. They all start laughing when I tell them the story, especially what Brian said, and they laugh even more when I say I'm going to keep it and call it Speed and teach it to do tricks. Speed? says Mary. Sure he can hardly stand up never mind run, the craitchur. They're all laughing at the two of us and all the time I'm hugging Speed because he's still squealing, in fact I'm nearly greetin' myself, and then they look at each other and stop laughing and say It's all right, Johnny, it's all right, ye can keep him so, but he'll have to stay out in the shed and eat scraps only for we'd be foolish indeed to let a sickly looking article like that inside the house.

There's a big lassie at the Sound School called Anna Lavelle who's always coming up and talking to me in the playground. She's got a nice face but she's a bit fat and she's got wee diddies under her blouse already and thick red beefy legs. The boys call her Fat Annie but not to her face.

I pass her daddy's field on the way back from school and there's a grey donkey in it sometimes.

One day we're talking about the time I saw her riding round the field on the donkey's back and she gave me a big wave and I waved back.

178

Ye can come over and have a ride on him yerself if ye like, she's saying now.

Big Nayliss and some of the boys are playing bools near us and when they hear this they burst out laughing.

Anna's face goes red and she walks away.

Ignorant, yiz are! she says to them. Pig ignorant, the lot o' yiz!

Big Nayliss comes over to me.

I'd say she'd be a grand ride herself, Scotty. Would ye say so?

I'm dead embarrassed. I don't know what to say. The other boys are killing themselves laughing.

That's no' very nice, is it?

It's all I can think of to say.

He's still watching Fat Annie walking across the yard.

Ah now, it's about as nice as ye'd get round here, I'd say.

They're roaring.

Speed follows me about all over the place and I'm fed up with people laughing at us and calling him a sorry-lookin' craitchur. So I'm going to train him to be a real dog like Black Bob, the sheepdog I love reading about in the *Weekly News* back in Paisley. Then I can be his master Andrew Glenn, with his black curly beard and shepherd's crook, striding the Selkirk hills with his faithful dog at his heel. The two of us are out in the barn and I've tied a bit of string to a stick to make a whip. Come on Speed, I say to him, we'll show them, and I try to crack the whip like a lion tamer though it doesn't crack at all, it hardly even makes a noise and the string just curls round the stick. Speed backs away from the whip and crouches looking up at me with his ears back and his eyes big and feart and you can see he doesn't like the look of it at all. It's a'right, Speed, I say, Ah'm gonnae train ye to do tricks. Sit, I say to him. Go on, down boy! But he just stands there looking glaikit and sorry for himself.

Come on, boy, sit! I try pressing the back of his legs with the edge of the stick because I saw in a comic once that's how you do it, but it's no good because when he sees the stick coming anywhere near him he backs away. Then I try looping the string round his back legs and pulling, another trick I read about in the comic, and after a while this trips him up and he sits down with a surprised look on his face. But he gets back up right away with that feart look in his eyes and scrabbles out of the loop and stands there panting. Down! I shout at him. Down boy! like a lion tamer, and try to crack my whip though it still won't crack. So I hit it against the wall to make the noise instead. Down, I shout again, and I'm getting angry at the way he just stands there scared and stupid-looking, Lie down! And I swing the whip at him and this time the string hits him, and he starts whimpering. It makes me angry to see he thinks I'm trying to hurt him. Shut up, I hiss at him in a tight whisper so my Auntie Mary won't hear us. Stop it, d'ye hear me? But he won't stop, he starts whimpering and squealing and cowering in a corner of the barn. And I keep banging the stick on the wall and then lashing at him with my whip to make him stop. Sometimes the string hits him and he whimpers and other times it's the stick that gets him and he starts yelping even louder and I'm getting feart my Auntie Mary will hear us and I'm wondering how hard I have to hit him to make him stop.

Stop it, I'm hissing at him. Stop that now, or I'll murder ye! Ya dope that ye are, ye're useless. Useless!

He's looking up at me with his dopey face and his eyes all big and scared and suddenly I think of the day my mammy got this old piano accordion secondhand from somewhere and brought it up to our house in Galloway Street and had me and Margaret standing up in front of the fireplace trying to play it. Go on, she kept saying, give us a tune now, but it was no good, we couldn't get anything out of it but noises. The Lord save us, ye're hopeless altogether, she said. Long piano fingers on ye too, the pair of ye, and ye can't even pick out a simple tune. Useless, that's what ye are!

Remembering this makes me feel ashamed. I throw the whip away.

It's a' right, Speed, I say, going down on my hunkers and rubbing my fingertips together to try and coax him, It's a'right. Come on boy, come here.

It's a while before he'll come to me, he's that feart, but when he does I sit on the ground and hug him that hard he starts whining again and Ah'm sorry, Speed, I say, Ah'm sorry, Ah'll never hit ye again, Ah promise, though it's hard for me to talk because I'm greetin' as well.

But the next time it's the same, and the next, and the time after that, and then one day I just give up. Some dogs can never learn tricks, no matter how hard you try.

The leaf's away and so's the bluebottle.

They're not in the water either. They must've blown away.

Then I see the bluebottle crawling along the edge of the barrel. It's not so blobby now, it's much drier. I can

181

see its wings and its shiny fat greeny behind. There's nothing blue about it.

It stops and tries out its wings. They seem to be stuck or tangled.

I try blowing on it to help it to get dry.

I blow too hard and it falls back in the water. I have to find another leaf to fish it out and slide it back onto the edge of the barrel.

It's drookit. It's all black and blobby again.

There's one boy at school who keeps himself to himself. He's a big beefy boy called Butler and he's better dressed than anybody else. There's no uniform at the Sound School, in fact one or two of the boys come to school in their bare feet, but Butler wears a jacket and sometimes even a tie. He seems nice enough though he doesn't talk much.

One morning when Sister Regis is leading the class in morning prayers I look out the window and there's Butler standing all by himself out in the playground. He's not doing anything, just standing there as if he's waiting for something. When I ask Brian Masterson later on he tells me Butler's a Protestant, the only one in the school, so he's excused prayers, it's all been fixed up with his mammy and daddy. And I'm thinking Lucky dog, skipping prayers every day.

I'm a bit jealous of Butler.

But later on I start feeling sorry for him stuck out there all by himself, especially on Holy Days when the statue of Our Lady is surrounded by flowers and wee candles and we're all inside singing one of my favourite hymns, like Queen of the May, and I'm putting my heart into it and getting that tingly feeling. Then I'll look out and see Butler mooching about in the yard. You'd think he'd be making faces at us, or jumping up and down or something, but no. He'll rub his hands together sometimes or just stand there looking up at the clouds passing by. You can see he's stuck for something to do. Sometimes he kicks a stone between his feet.

I wonder if he knows I'm watching him.

Speed's been looking scruffy. His white coat's got all grey with wee bits of dirt and fluff all over it and Auntie Mary's been passing remarks, saying It'd break yer heart the way that dirty-looking mutt goes mooning about the place, God save the mark he's no oil painting at the best of times, a good wash and scrub is what he needs. So one day I walk him down to the stream where Mickey Tom takes me fishing sometimes. We walk along the bank following the water down to a place where it starts to level out into pools and when we get to one that looks deep enough I throw a stick in and shout Fetch, Speed, go on boy! But Speed just cringes there looking up at me with his head to one side and his tail curled under him. So I pick him up and say Good boy, Speed, it's a'right, it's a'right, and pat his head so he calms down and then I heave him into the pool.

It's dead funny the way his hair flattens into his head and him paddling away like mad this way and that trying to get out. At first he comes back to the bottom of the bank where I'm standing but I stamp my feet at him and shout No! Ye're to stay in there and get clean! So he paddles away to where the water falls into the pool but there's big rocks there and they're all wet and slippy when he tries to climb up on them and you can see he's feart of the water splashing down on his head.

Then he swims to the other end where the water drops over the edge but he turns back from there pretty quick. I'm watching all this from the bank and having a good laugh at him, he looks that comical with his wee head all shrunk and bony and his eyes bulging out twice their size and him whimpering. Then I see he can't make it up the sides of the bank because the rock is too steep and smooth for his paws to get a grip on and I start worrying how is he going to get out. So I get down on my hands and knees on the bank and say Come on Speed, come on, up here boy! and hold out my hand to him but it's no good, he's too far below me and his paws just scrape and slip on the rock. Sometimes he makes it halfway up, he's that desperate, but then he just slides back down into the water and has to start all over again. He's shivering now and he looks worn out. By this time I'm getting feart myself. I stand up to see if there's anybody about so I can shout for help. But there's not a soul in the fields around us and though I can see one or two people walking out on the strand below they're miles away and they'd never hear me. The sky is getting dark and I can feel a chill in the air and I'm starting to panic. I lie face down on the bank right on the edge and stretch down as far as I can but I still can't reach him. The ground is cold and damp under me and I get as good a grip as I can on a clump of grass and try to dig into the earth with my left toe because I've got my right leg halfway down the bank braced to keep my balance. I slide my right hand as far down the wet rock as I dare and pray he'll make it up high enough so I can grab his paw or something. But even if I can, who's to say I'll be able to pull him up and out without falling in myself? I can't swim and I'm terrified the two of us are going to drown out here in the middle of nowhere. But I can't just leave him to die. It was me that threw him in, it would be a mortal sin, I'd be damned for ever. Oh God, I'm praying, please let him be a'right, please let him get out safe, Ah'll be good, Ah'll be a good boy till the end of my days. Promise. And whether it's me praying or desperation or just sheer luck, Speed scrabbles up the side far enough so I can grab on to his paw and slowly, slowly, hardly daring to breathe, I haul him squealing up onto the bank beside me.

He stands there drookit and shivering with his hair plastered down on his white skinny body so he looks more like a drowned rat than a dog. Even when he shakes himself off he's soaking wet but still I wrap my arms round him and hug him as hard as I can to my chest so I get soaked as well. He's whimpering and yelping and I'm greetin' and saying Ah'm sorry, Ah'm sorry. I know I'll be in trouble with Auntie Mary for getting my clothes soaking wet but I'm that relieved I don't care.

What's a few hard words and black looks when you could have drowned and died in mortal sin and been condemned for all eternity to the fires of hell?

I'm getting worried about Speed. He's been mooching and moping about the house and when I try to get him to run along with me he only runs a few yards then stands there panting and looking pathetic with his legs splayed and his tongue hanging out.

Auntie Mary's standing at the door talking to Aunt Nancy one day when Speed starts coughing and heaving in the yard outside and this yellowy stuff comes out of his mouth. It's not like vomit, it's all in one piece, nearly solid, like a long lumpy sausage.

185

That dog's for the high jump, Mary says. He's had his chips, if you ask me.

I'd say he's a goner all right, says Aunt Nancy, shaking her head. God help him.

Aunt Nancy's good-hearted. She knows about dogs.

Didn't I tell ye that the first time I clapped eyes on him? Auntie Mary says to me. From the day I saw him I said he was a sickly-looking article.

Ah, God love him, says Aunt Nancy. Ye'd feel sorry for him, the craitchur.

I don't know who she means, me or Speed.

We'll bring Martin Tony up and look at him, she says.

They stare at each other and nod.

When I come home from school the next day there's no sign of Speed.

Arra how would I know where he is? says Auntie Mary.

She knows. I can tell from her face.

Away ye go down and ask Aunt Nancy. And don't be bothering me wit' yer questions.

And down I go, though I know before Aunt Nancy tells me that Speed's gone away and he'll never come back.

Martin Tony took one look at him, *ahashki*, says Aunt Nancy, and there was nothing else to do only put the poor craitchur out of his misery.

I go outside and crouch down by the doorstep stroking Old Banger and trying hard not to think about Speed.

Aunt Nancy has always had a dog. It's always the same kind of black and white sheepdog and she always calls it Banger. Bang-gur she pronounces it. When it gets old it becomes Old Banger and after a while she gets a new pup she calls Bangeen, which is Irish for Wee Banger. Then when the old dog dies Bangeen becomes the new Banger.

Aunt Nancy comes out and tells me I can come down and play with Old Banger any time I want.

I think about Speed dogpaddling in the rock pool the time I threw him in. His eyes huge and feart in his skinny head.

I hope to God they didn't drown him.

My Auntie Mary has funny ways about her sometimes. Half the time she'll be nice enough and then other times she'll boss me about and call me a latchyko or an amathon whenever I do something wrong. Amathon more than the maiden, she says, or something like that. It's Irish. I don't understand it but I've heard my mammy calling me that before so I know she's not singing my praises. And then other times she'll act like a wee lassie, giggling and saying daft things.

I think when she was lodging with us in Galloway Street she took a fancy to big Ainas McNulty from number six, because she keeps talking about him.

Oh a fine-looking fella, she'll say to the Yank, and the grand gentlemanly ways he has about him.

She's sitting up in her bed late this day because she's been feeling poorly.

How would it be, she says to me, if Ainas was in here beside me now, wouldn't that be grand?

I just shrug my shoulders. I don't know what she means.

D'you think would he give me a baby?

I have no idea what baby she's talking about. I try to picture big Ainas McNulty walking over to her carrying a wee baby and leaning down to hand it to her.

Aye, I suppose he would, I say at last.

D'you think so? she says and she giggles like a wee lassie getting a birthday present. D'you think he would? Well, you might be right. I think he had a soft spot for me, the same Ainas.

Where would he get it? I ask her.

She looks at me.

Where would he get what?

The baby. The baby he's gonnae give you. Where would he get it?

She stares at me and bursts out laughing.

The Lord save us don't you know anything at all? Are ye that ignorant? Do ye not know about that little – polisman's whistle ye have between yer legs? What d'ye think it's for?

I'm embarrassed she's talking about these things and I can feel my ears burning but I'm going to show her I'm not that ignorant.

Aye, well if I've got a whistle, you've got a slit!

Oh have I now? she says. And how would you know? Do ye be spying on me, or what?

She's got this sly look on her face with her eyes glittering and her head cocked to one side the way I can't tell if she's pleased or angry. I just stand there because I can't think what else to say.

Ah, go on wit' you, she says at last. Let you pick up that pot from under the bed and take it outside and empty it, she says, It's all you're good for.

She's got this old saucepan she keeps under the bed and uses as a chanty sometimes during the night. But she empties it herself. She's never asked me to do it before.

Ah'm no' doin' that, I tell her. That's no' my job.

On ye go, she says, and less of yer cheek. Just take it outside and empty it. Go on wit' ye now, I'll be getting up in a minute.

She throws back the bedclothes and I can't help seeing her long legs white and bare and a dark shadow at the top where her nightgown is rumpled and lying half open. She makes a great show of pulling it around her to cover herself up.

What're you standing there gawping at? she says. Do you want to see me, is that it? Is it spying on me you are?

She lies there staring at me and half smiling and she's got the sly look again and I'm excited and feart at the same time. I don't want to empty her smelly old chanty but I'm feart to defy her and I'm feart to stay in that room. So I reach under the bed and grab the saucepan by the handle and pull it out dead slow, thinking it's got pee in it and I don't want it to spill. But it's worse than that, it's got wee skittery keichs in it and a terrible smell. I'm that scunnered I'm nearly choking. I run outside and fling the whole thing, saucepan and all, out into the long grass behind the house. But the bad smell's still there in my nose and the back of my throat as I lean on one hand against the side of the house taking big deep breaths and staring down to the strand below, though all I can see is her long pale legs and the dark place under her nightgown.

The bluebottle's dried out again. I blew on it to help it but I held an old cigarette packet behind it this time so it wouldn't fall back in the barrel.

It's trying out its wings. It moves them slowly up and

*down, then crawls a bit further along the edge. Then it
tries them again.*

*I don't think it can fly. I might keep it as a pet and
feed it crumbs. It'd be company for me.*

*It tries again. The wings whir this time. Maybe they
work after all.*

*Just when I'm thinking I might have to dunk it in the
water again, it takes off.*

It's gone. Just like that.

*After all I've done for it, you'd think it could've
stayed.*

I'm sitting in the train with my Auntie Mary and I'm all
excited because this is the day I go back to Scotland.
I'm wearing the outfit Auntie Mary bought me in
Dublin the day we arrived. It was money my mammy
gave her to buy me clothes. It's a funny greenybrown
jerkin with matching short trousers and this is the first
time I've worn it.

My mammy's been writing back and forth to Auntie
Mary and at last it's all fixed up: she'll be waiting to
meet us when the train gets to Dublin.

How long will it be now? I keep asking Auntie Mary
but all she'll say is Amn't I fed up telling you?

She's been in a bad mood for days, snappy and
sarcastic.

He won't be back a week before he'll forget all about
us, she said to the Yank, who came with us as far as
Westport to see us off.

Ah, sure that's the way of the world, *ahashki*, said
the Yank.

She was nearly greetin', standing there on the platform waving as the train pulled away.

The journey takes ages and after a while Auntie

190

Mary falls asleep and I've got nothing else to do but sit staring out the window at the fields and hills sliding past. I'm wondering how it'll be when I see my mammy. I've never been away from her this long before, it's been months and months, and I don't know how I'm supposed to act. In the pictures you always see people hugging and kissing on railway platforms but we never do that in our family. Except for my daddy, he's always hugging and kissing us when he's drunk though maybe that doesn't count. Or else he goes round shaking hands with everybody. He looks at you dead sincere with his eyes shining and sticks out his hand. Put it there, pal, he says. When he's like that he'll even try and kiss my mammy as well. Ah Margaret, Margaret, he'll say, the best in the world. It's the only time we ever hear him saying her name. And she never calls him Mick to his face, or to us either, only when she's talking to somebody else and being polite. Everybody else that comes up to our house calls him Mick, though Michael is what Miss O'Neill called him one day years ago when all the parents came visiting at St James's. I was only about six at the time and I was a bit worried to tell the truth, with him being Only a labourer, as my mammy always says, and Miss O'Neill a teacher and kinda posh. But the two of them stood there blethering away quite the thing. Then I heard Miss O'Neill talking to Mother Stanislaus afterwards. Did you meet John's father? Miss O'Neill said. Michael Boyle? Oh a very nice young man. A charming young man. It's funny to hear somebody calling my daddy young, because to me he's quite old, but I'm relieved when she says that about him being charming because it must mean she doesn't care he's only a labourer. It's true enough, I suppose, people like my daddy. You can see it in their faces when they come up to the house. You can see it in the way they talk to him.

Not my mammy though. Whenever he tries to give her a kiss she looks dead embarrassed and pushes him away.

For God's sake, man, she says to him, Have ye no shame?

So what am I supposed to do when I see her?

I better not try and give her a kiss.

So will I just shake hands with her or what? And what will I say to her after all this time?

I can't say, Put it there pal.

Maybe I should just say, Hello Mum, how are you?

Mammy sounds a bit babyish, and I'm a big boy now.

I hope to God I don't act daft and make a fool of myself.

But this all goes for nothing when we get off the train in Dublin because as soon as I see her standing there at the barrier I'm racing towards her like a big wean and shouting *Mammy Mammy Mammy* and when I get near enough I jump up into her arms and throw mine round her neck. And she nuzzles my head and gives me a big squeeze and pats me on the back and says, My, my, my, what a welcome! I'm out of breath at ye!

I hold her hand as we walk through the crowds and I'm not embarrassed at all the way I thought I would be. My mammy's talking away to Auntie Mary saying Lord above, hasn't he grown? and telling me I've got an Irish accent now, I sound like a real Mayo man.

I can't get over it, she keeps saying, He's pure plain spoken. But in the name o' God, she says, where did ye get that quarelookin' outfit he has on him?

That's moleshkin, Auntie Mary says. I got it in

Cleary's. It's good hardwearing shtuff, they say. The real McCoy.

Well did ye ever hear the like? says my mammy. Moleskin Joe, they'll be calling ye now. Moleskin Joe, I swear to God.

The two of them are having a good laugh at me but I don't care. In fact I'm only half listening because all I can think about is seeing her face again and how glad I am to be going home and isn't it funny to think this is the first time I can remember hugging my mammy?

Foreigner

My Irish accent is getting me into trouble. My mammy's pleased because I'm pure plain-spoken now, as she calls it, and she never had much time for the Scottish accent anyhow. But Margaret and Frankie only laugh at me and take the mickey.

When we get back to Galloway Street my mammy gets out her purse to buy us all ice-cream from the van because it's a special day with me coming home and when I say I want a treepenny one Frankie walks about making funny faces and saying A treepenny one, a treepenny one! in a daft posh voice. It's worse when my daddy comes in from work. I notice him giving me funny looks when he hears me talking. At first I think maybe he thinks I'm just kidding him on so I laugh and tell him No, no, that's the way I do talk now, Daddy, honest to God. He's Irish himself so you'd think he'd be pleased. But not a bit of it. By the look on his face you'd think somebody had died or some other terrible thing had happened.

Are you John, or what are ye at all? he says. Ah don't know what's come over ye son but Ah wish to God ye would cut out that rubbage and get back to talking right, the way ye did before.

He still says rubbage, I notice, though I don't pass any remarks.

It's as bad when I'm back at St James's. We're doing spelling in Big Bill's class and I'm standing up spelling 'accommodation'. I'm good at spelling so I get it right except I pronounce the A's the Irish way, which is ah, not ay.

What's all this 'ah' business? Big Bill asks.

Oh that's the way they do say it in Ireland, I tell him, dead chuffed because I've travelled and seen a bit of the world.

Oh is it now? says Big Bill in a very sarky tone of voice. Well maybe you haven't noticed, laddie, but you're not in Ireland now.

And the whole class has a good laugh at me and I sit down with my ears burning. It's a hard thing to come back home and feel like a foreigner in your own country.

It gets me thinking about the way my mammy talks.

Let ye be getting up now, she'll say when she's getting us up in the morning, and get yerselves dressed. And let ye be quick about it or ye'll be late for school.

Let ye.

Let ye go down now to Galbraith's, she'll say other times, and get me a loaf of bread.

Nobody else's mammy talks like that. It's not her fault; she's Irish, she wasn't brought up in Scotland and neither was my daddy, but sometimes I wish they could just talk like everybody else.

In Achill I was different because I was Scottish and now I'm back in Scotland I'm different because I sound Irish.

It seems to me I'm a foreigner wherever I go.

195

*　　*　　*

I'm down in the close one night looking out for Wullie or Toono but there's no sign of them. There's nobody out the backdoor either. It's dark and empty out there. I look out the front and see some boys from the end of the street bunched beside the lamppost outside number eight. They're cooried in together under the light, whispering and sniggering.

Then they go in the close.

The street's deserted. It must be a fight or something. I run down there to see.

The close at number eight is empty but I can hear noises out the backdoor. I can hardly see, it's that dark after the lights in the street, but there's a gang of boys gathered outside one of the coalbunkers.

It's not a fight, they're too quiet. It must be something else. Something secret.

Whit is it? I whisper to a boy at the back.

It's Toono, he says.

I can't see the boy's face. He's not looking at me, he's up on tiptoe, straining to see past the boys in front. They're all squeezed in in front of the coalbunker.

Whit's he daein'? I ask.

Ssh!

I try to push in further, get nearer so I can see. But I can only hear the whispering and scuffling inside the bunker and the boys round me breathing and swallowing.

Then I hear a lassie giggling, trying to hold it back.

He's got Kathy Gibson in there, the boy near me whispers. He's gonnae ride 'ur!

It's Flash Anderson. I'm getting used to the light now. I can see his eyes glittering and this slack smile he's got. His mouth's all wet and slavery. He looks dead excited.

So am I. Kathy Gibson is a big lassie with fair hair from the end of the street. I don't know much about her except she's a Proddy and she's older than me.

Hey Toono, I hiss from the back, whit're ye daein'?

I'm chuffed because I'm in Toono's gang. And I'm getting my Scottish accent back. I try to make it sound gallous but it comes out wrong, a bit dopey.

Who's askin'?

It's Toono all right. I know his voice.

It's me. Boyle. Whit're ye daein', Toono?

Whid'ye think Ah'm daein'?

He sounds that casual Flash bursts out laughing and somebody hisses at him to shoosh.

I'm embarrassed because I asked a stupid question. I need to say something tough, show I'm not a sissy.

Are ye ridin' 'ur, Toono?

I can hardly say the words, my throat's that dry. It's the first time I've ever said that word. It's a sin.

No' yet. Ah'm ticklin' her fanny.

No' yet! I don't know what to say back. Nobody else says anything. We're all squeezed together there in the dark, hardly breathing, straining to see something, straining to hear, imagining what Toono's doing to Kathy Gibson. Wishing it was us instead of him. Even though I know I could never do it, not with other boys there. I'd be ashamed.

Toono doesn't care. Lucky dog. That's the way he is. Doesn't give a tinker's curse.

Gonnae leave some for us, eh Toono? somebody says, then others join in:

Aye. Eh?

Gonnae?

Be a pal!

Maybe we'll all get a shot! I'm that jittery, I'm giddy.
I can hardly breathe. My wullie's all stiff and sore.

Aye that'll be right, Toono says, dead gallous. Away
yeez go and gi'e's peace.

Kathy Gibson says something then and Shoosh, he
whispers to her, shoosh. 'S a'right, hen. 'S a'right.

The next thing is, we hear Mrs Gibson shouting out
her window. The Gibsons live at number fifteen, away
down the end of the street on the other side but you
can still hear her.

Kathy? Kathy Gibson! Come up the hoose!

Then she shouts down to somebody in the street.

Haw, Sandra! Hiv ye seen oor Kathy? Tell 'ur tae
come up the hoose this minnit!

She knows. You can tell.

Flash looks at me and makes a face as if to say,
Sumdy's fur the high jump.

Kathy Gibson says something, I can't hear what,
she's whispering, but it sounds angry and feart. We
can hear Toono telling her, Shoosh, shoosh, it's a'right.
But they keep arguing. More scuffling, then Toono
again:

A'right, let 'er oot! She's g'n up the hoose.
Cummoan, oot the wey!

He sounds really cheesed off. The crowd in front of
me breaks up and Kathy Gibson pushes through. She
doesn't look at anybody, just pushes past us, combing
her hair with her fingers.

I hardly get time to see her face. She looks dead pale,
her mouth all tight and wee.

We're all trying to ask Toono what it was like,

what he was doing to her in there, but he's raging mad at us.

A' that racket yeez wur makin', he says. It's nae wunner 'ur aul' yin fun' oot!

He walks away up the street on his own and nobody dares to follow him. Nobody's talking much any more though some boys are still sniggering and whispering. But we all go dead quiet when we hear the racket coming from the Gibsons' house. Kathy Gibson is getting a terrible battering from her mammy. We stand there listening to the slaps and shouts and screams then we get a bit ashamed and feart and start creeping away in case we might get the blame. There's a loud crash when something tips over and smashes in the Gibsons' kitchen and after that things get quieter. But even when I'm back in our close at number four I can still hear Kathy Gibson greetin' and moaning *Ah'm sorry mammy, Ah'm sorry, Ah'll no' dae it again, honest, Ah'll no' dae it again . . . !*

We've got a record player.

I've been pestering my mammy for weeks to get a secondhand one because I know she'll never buy anything new if she can help it. Now she's got us one through an advertisement she saw in a paper shop in Well Street.

The trouble is, we haven't got any records.

Then my mammy remembers the man she bought it from was selling records as well. They're Johnny Ray records, she tells me.

Is he no' that guy that starts greetin' when he's singin' 'Cry'?

Yes, I believe that's the one.

Ah don't think much o' him.

Arra what's the matter wit' ye? I'm not that gone on him myself, but do ye want records, or do ye not?

I suppose Johnny Ray's better than nothing. So we phone up from the phonebox near Jimmy Canning's and she gets the man to lower the price if we take the lot. She gives me the right money and tells me where I'm to go.

It's in a row of tenements just before you get to Well Street. The man lets me in and we go through a kitchen that's a bit barelooking with hardly any furniture and into the back room. There's not much here either, only boxes and books and the only thing on the mantelpiece is a wee framed photo of a woman. One of the boxes has got a pile of records on top of it. Some are in square paper covers and others are just loose.

It's a'right son, the man says when I ask. There's wan or two wi' their covers missin' but they're a' in good condition, Ah kin promise ye that.

I'm embarrassed he might think I was complaining. I only said it for something to say. He starts sliding the records out of their covers and holding them up to the light from the window to show me there are no scratches. I must say they look nice, black and smooth and shiny with the wee fans of light spreading out from the label to the edge. At the same time he keeps talking about Johnny Ray, what a marvellous singer he is and how he puts that much feeling into his songs. And watching this man, the way he handles his records dead slow and careful, holy even, like Father Murphy with the Blessed Host on the altar, I think, Whit's he sellin' them fur if he loves them that much? But I don't ask, because there's an awful sad feeling about this half-empty house and this man talking to a complete stranger, a wee boy, about things that mean a lot to him, you can tell from his voice. Maybe he just wants to sell his records, but I don't think so. Whatever it is, it's not that.

D'ye like Johnny Ray, son? Urr ye a fan?

He catches me by surprise and I nearly tell him no, it's just that we need records to go with the record player, but something makes me change my mind.

Naw . . . well, no' exactly a *fan*, Ah don't know enough aboot 'um, but Ah like his songs. Ah really like that 'Cry'.

Dae ye son?

He smiles at me, a sad smile, and I'm glad I told him a lie.

Aye. So diz ma mammy.

Och that's too bad, son, he says. 'Cry' wiz ma favourite an' a', but it's aboot the only wan that's no' here.

He's looking over at the photo on the mantelpiece.

Aye. That yin got broke.

But all the other big hits are there, he tells me, 'Ain't Misbehavin'' and 'Just Walking in the Rain' and a lot more he mentions that I've never heard of and I'm nodding and smiling and hoping he doesn't ask any more questions because I don't want this man to find out I know nothing about Johnny Ray.

I walk back to Galloway Street carrying my new records in a cardboard box. I walk dead slow and careful because this is my Johnny Ray collection. I can hardly wait to listen to them on our new record player. We might even be able to buy 'Cry' somewhere. Then we'll have a full set.

It's the Sunday after Christmas, a frosty day but sunny with blue skies, and I'm sitting by the fire in the kitchen with my presents. There's nobody in except my mammy doing her ironing at the table and wee Bernard sleeping in his cot. My daddy's at High Mass with the other weans but I don't have to go because I was serving the eight o'clock.

This year I got nearly everything I wanted: a cricket bat and the *Oor Wullie* annual, a draughts set, a Fair Isle pullover, a pair of gloves, and some bars of chocolate and a packet of dolly mixtures.

I'm reading the *Oor Wullie* annual and eating the dolly mixtures. Every so often I look up at my cricket bat that I've put in the corner of the fireplace. I wanted a cricket bat so I could learn cricket and be like Harry Wharton and the gang at Greyfriars School. I'm thinking maybe I can start a team in Galloway Street, once I've learned how to play, then I can teach everybody else and be the captain.

Oor Wullie's up to some mischief with Fat Boab and Soapy Soutar and they get nabbed by PC Murdoch, but Wullie's come up with a dodge so he gets away with it and the other two get the blame and at the end he's sitting on his bucket as usual, chortling. I can't help laughing myself.

What're ye laughin' at? my mammy asks.

It's ma *Oor Wullie* book, I tell her.

The Lord save us, is it that funny?

Aye, well . . . the *Oor Wullie* stories hardly ever make ye laugh, no' oot loud anyway, but this yin's quite funny. Fat Boab and Soapy try an' play this trick on Wullie, but Wullie sees through it an'—

She laughs.

202

The Lord save us, she says, No need to tell me the whole story. Just you sit there and enjoy it, son.

Son. She's in a good mood. I think she quite likes ironing; it's the only time you ever hear her humming.

She's not humming now, but she looks as if she's enjoying the sound of the bells ringing at the Protestant church round the corner in Underwood Road.

I look round the room, at the cheery fire in the grate, my cricket bat standing there in the corner, the wood all blond and shiny, and my mammy at the table ironing and listening to the bells. The sun is blazing in at the window and the light on her face makes it pale and soft and rested, and watching her I realize that sometimes my mammy can look quite beautiful.

Mammy, I say to her, d'ye know whit?

What is it? she says.

Ah think this is the happiest day a ma life.

It just comes out like that; I can't help it.

She looks at me.

What d'ye mean, *ahashki*? I thought yer first communion was supposed to be the happiest day of yer life.

Aye, Ah know. But this is better.

The Lord save us, she says, I don't see what's so good about it.

Well Ah mean, it's Christmas 'n that and I've got the *Oor Wullie* annual Ah wantit and a big packet of dolly mixtures an' ma bat 'n everythin' . . .

That's all I say but I mean a lot more; I mean the sun shining and the bells ringing and the fire crackling in the grate and the baby sleeping and me and my mammy there in the house, just the two of us, and everything quiet and peaceful.

She starts laughing.

Begod, she says, isn't it happy for ye, if an oul' comic book and a few sweets is all it takes to cheer ye up? Ah well, ye're easy pleased, *ahashki*. I'll say that for ye. Ye're easy pleased, right enough.

1952

We're in Big Bill's class the day the Marist Brother comes to talk to us. The Marist Brothers are an order of monks and they're coming round St James's to see if any boy among us might have the vocation, which is the Call from God to give up thy worldly goods and go and be a monk. The Marist Brother seems nice enough and he tells us all about the Good Works that his order does and how it's a hard life but a rewarding one for a boy of the right calibre.

When he's finished Big Bill says Hands up any boy who thinks he might be interested and we all look around because nobody wants to go first but the only hand that goes up is McGovern's. And we're all amazed because McGovern nearly got expelled from St James's last year for waving his wullie at the lassies in the playground and he's been in Big Bill's black books ever since so we reckon he's just being a sook.

All right McGovern, Big Bill says, your interest has been noted, you can put your hand down. He gives McGovern a dirty look but you can see he doesn't like to say anything in front of the Marist Brother.

He looks around at the rest of us.

What about our altarboys, no flicker of interest there? John? he says, meaning me, because if he likes you he calls you by your first name. What about you, Pat? Or you, Hugh?

To tell the truth I'm quite interested because I like Father Murphy and sometimes wonder what it would be like to be a priest like him but of course I've never told anybody. So I look at Foley and McDowall and they look at me and we shrug, might as well, and put our hands up. And so do Duignan and Higgins and Kiernan.

Grand, grand, says the Marist Brother, and he tells us of course it's early days yet, we'll have plenty of time to pray to Our Lord for guidance and never fear, He'll send us a Sign if we have the vocation. In the meantime, he says, I'll leave you these leaflets that tell you all about our training college in Newbury. Any boy who's interested just leave your name with Mr Campbell and the Order will be in touch with you, never fear.

After he leaves we get a few minutes to look at the leaflets and I begin to think McGovern must have seen them before because the photos show the training college is a grand building in some kind of country estate down in England, with playing fields and cricket nets and all your orders. It reminds me of the posh English public schools I read about in library books, like Greyfriars School where Billy Bunter goes and Harry Wharton and Johnny Bull with their Indian pal Hurree Jamset Ram Singh, who would surely take one look at this place and say The luxuriousness is terrific. I'm thinking it will be no great sacrifice for me to give up my worldly goods in exchange for all this, but I try to keep the thought out of my head in case Our Lord hears it and decides I'm not worthy.

So I'm sitting there hoping the Call will come to me and I can see myself already, asleep in the dorm after Lights Out or strolling in the quad or down to the Tuck Shop with my chums or even going Out of Bounds and shouting *Wizard wheeze, chaps!* or maybe *Cave, Beak!* if I see the teacher coming, though I always wonder where the cave is that they're shouting about because nobody ever seems to go there. But of course I'll always remember Galloway Street and come back here for the Hols so I can call my mammy Mater and my daddy Pater and lord it over my wee sister and wee brothers and the rest of the scruff in this dump of a place.

John, come in here a minute.

It's my mammy calling me from the big room. I'm in the kitchen reading my *Wizard* and enjoying a bit of peace with the new baby sleeping in her shawl on the bed and wee Bernard quiet in his cot.

Whit is it?

Never mind that, just come in here and I'll show you.

It's her hissy voice. I'm in trouble by the sound of it.

She's standing by the window with the wardrobe door open and she's got a jacket over her arm. Maybe she's found something in my pockets.

She holds out a wee brown envelope.

Would ye look at that!

It's a pay packet with my daddy's name in writing on it, M. Boyle and some printing: Hours Worked, Overtime, Bonus, Total.

I don't know what I'm supposed to be looking at.

Whit're ye showin' me fur?

Look at that. There, at the top. Look.

She taps her fingernail on a figure somebody's written next to Total. It's hard to read because it's a bit messy but it says seven pounds fourteen shillings.

I still don't get it.

Would ye believe that man? she's hissing at me.

Who? Whit is it?

Arra who d'ye think it is? Yer daddy, God forgive him. Who else would it be? What other man would take the food out of his own family's mouth to go boozing in the pubs? Out getting stupid drunk instead of feeding his family? Well the curse o' God on him, for he's no kind of a man at all that would do that.

When she curses like this her eyes glitter and her face gets all tight and strained like a balloon ready to burst and I'm always feart something terrible is going to happen.

Ehm . . . are ye sure? Ah mean, how d'ye know?

Arra have ye no eyes in your head, or what's the matter wit' ye at all? Can ye not see where's he's been changing the figures on his paypacket! Look at that seven, he's changed that from, Jesus Mary and Joseph, was it nine pound? Two pound he's stolen from his own wife and children! Would ye believe any man could do such a thing?

I hate her talking to me about him like this, in her tight, hissy voice, but I can see what she means. Somebody's been fiddling with the nine and changing it into a seven by rubbing out the loop and straightening out the tail. But it's a mess, he's used a dirty rubber or his finger so it's all smudgy then he's written over the seven with a biro. There's another seven on the packet, it's in the date, and anybody can see it's different writing.

Well, she says, what d'ye think o' that man now? I

207

hope ye're proud of him. How am I supposed to feed six o' ye with seven pound a week after paying the rent on this house? By God, it would be hard enough with nine pound, but now . . . Does he want us to starve and end up in the poorhouse, is that what he wants? Because that's where we'll end up, I swear to God. And where'll he be then? Living in the Model in Well Street, that's where he'll be, with his drinking pals from the pub, and bad cess to the lot o' them. Let him see how he likes it then, because there's only one place left for him after that and that's straight down to the gutter and the pit of Hell. And may God forgive me for saying it, but that's where he belongs.

The new baby starts whimpering next door and it sets wee Bernard off greetin' in his cot and makes my mammy get even angrier.

D'ye see? she hisses at me. Ye see what that man's made me do now? Jesus Mary and Joseph that's the baby wakened up and the child as well and between the two of them we won't get a moment's peace. Let ye get in there and try rocking him, maybe he'll go back to sleep with God's help.

I go through to the kitchen and start rocking the cot, to and fro. She picks up wee Irene in her shawl and walks up and down with her, saying, Wheesht, wheesht. She's still holding the envelope.

I'll go mad one o' these days, she says, I will, honest to God. D'ye see the state I'm in at the lot of ye? I'm up to High Doh at ye all, and I can't put up with it any more. God Almighty, what kind of a woman could put up with this without going out of her mind?

I'm rocking the cot even harder now, *toandfro toandfro*, but wee Bernard's still greetin'.

I get feart when my mammy talks like this but I can't

get away so I just kid on I'm listening. I concentrate on the rhythm of the cot rocking *toandfro toandfro toandfro toandfro* and try hard to think about something else. I think about the story I was reading in the *Wizard* about Wilson the great athlete. Wilson wears woolly longjohns and trains with boulders instead of dumbbells and lives all by himself in a mystery cave somewhere in the hills and I'm thinking it must be great to be like Wilson, with no boozing father or hissing mother or greetin' weans to disturb your peace of mind and a wee place all your own that nobody knows about where you can go and lie low when bad things happen in the world.

Big Bill's reading out the results of the tests. He reads out our marks for English, history, geography, arithmetic and religious knowledge. I've got high marks for everything except arithmetic because I'm hopeless at sums.

54.5 per cent. So you just about scraped a pass, Big Bill says.

He smiles and tells us he's done enough work marking all our papers and adding up the totals so we have to help him with the next step, working out our average percentage mark to see who's Top Boy or Top Girl in the class.

Off you go, then, Big Bill says, and bring your papers out here to my desk when you're finished.

I copy down all my marks in a column and start adding them up though I'm not sure what you do after that. I can never understand averages. The time Big Bill explained it and asked Is that clear? everybody said Yes sir, and so did I.

Not wanting to look stupid in front of the class.

Even the adding up is quite hard because of the decimals. That's another thing I can never work out. I try hard to concentrate on the figures on the paper in front of me but it's no good, they don't mean anything. It's not like words; you can just look at a word and you know what it means. Or you can work it out from the other words around it, or look it up in the dictionary. Words are easy, except in arithmetic where it's words like fractions and decimals and percentages and averages. Not like words at all, more like figures or symbols. Like a foreign language only worse, because even the words foreigners say in comics, like *Sacre bleu!* or *Donner und Blitzen!* make more sense to me than fractions and decimals. I look across at Hugh McDowall and he's sitting there quite the thing working out his sum and smiling away to himself. You'd think he was playing a game. Lucky dog, he's good at sums.

Because I keep getting the decimals wrong I have to rub out the total twice and that smudges the paper. It reminds me of my daddy's paypacket.

I'm not even sure any more about things I thought I knew. What is .5 per cent? What does that mean?

I get the sum right at last, at least I think so. But what comes after that? Is it division or multiplication?

I think you divide the total, 417.5 per cent, by 5, because there are five subjects.

Or maybe you multiply them and then divide by 100, because it's a percentage?

Or the other way about, divide 100 by 417.5 per cent?

But how can you, if it doesn't go?

And where does the five come in?

My hands are oozing sweat and they keep sticking

to the paper. Hugh McDowall gets up to take out his paper and I sneak a look sideyways to see what kind of sum he's done.

A division.

I knew that, I think, and I start doing the division but I'm dead worried because McDowall's finished already and here's me just starting. And it's hard to concentrate because other boys and lassies are getting up and marching out to Big Bill with their papers and coming back and sitting down whispering and laughing. They're happy because they've finished the sum and soon it'll be the holidays and Big Bill's in a good mood. The division is hard because of the decimal point but I'm trying my best to go fast, not to be last. And I keep making mistakes so I rub out and smudge, then try to write over it, digging the point in hard till ohmyGod it goes through the page and my whole paper's a mess and I'm thinking, I'll never get this done.

Then I notice the class has gone dead quiet. I look up and see them all half-looking at me and half at Big Bill. Big Bill's standing there at his desk staring straight at me with a sorrowful look on his face and I realize the noise has stopped because everybody else has finished and brought their paper out to him, even slowcoaches like Kiernan and McKean.

Big Bill shakes his head. It's a shame, isn't it? he says. Top Boy in the exam and he can't even work out his own average. Bring your paper out here, he says, sounding scunnered and fed-up. The bell will be going any minute.

Mortified I trudge out there and hand him my paper. He looks at it and shakes his head again and sighs like a man reading tragic news. I've a good mind, he says, to get Kiernan or McKean out here to work out your average for you on the board. But we haven't got time for that. Your average is 83.5 per cent. Top Boy in the class. I hope you're proud of yourself.

Foley giggles as I walk back to my desk but hardly anybody joins in. It's even worse, they're all just sitting there dead quiet. I've embarrassed the whole class and they'll all hate me now because I've put Big Bill in a bad mood. McColl turns round and smiles at me as if to cheer me up but he's shaking his head as well as if to say, Ah John, ye're a hopeless case.

He's right. What's the use of being Top Boy if you're no good at sums?

I sit staring at my desk, my face burning, and I'm praying the bell will ring. Soon they start talking and laughing again but it's all outside me, I only half hear them. I just sit and stare at the white inkwell on my desk till it gets all blurry and seems to float up slowly out of its round hole and swim in the mist in front of my eyes.

Me and Toono and Charlie have been following the pipe band down Underwood Road. It's better fun than the Orange Walk: there's never any trouble and it doesn't matter if you're a Catholic or a Protestant. And the music is much better. Whenever I hear the bagpipes I get a wee shiver down my back and it makes my skin tingle. The sad tunes always make me feel like greetin'. When I hear the pipes and drums and watch the big Highlanders marching along with their kilts swinging and their buckles and daggers glinting, and the pipe major up the front joogling his silver mace, I get a choky feeling in my throat and I'm dead proud to be Scottish.

Except I'm not Scottish, not really. Sometimes I'm ashamed of our Irish name. It's not even one of the nice Irish names, like Kelly or Flanagan or Flaherty. Boyle: what kind of a name is that? I wonder what it would be like to have a real Scottish name like Rob Roy McGregor or Rory McPherson or Alistair Campbell. They're great names, with a kind of noble sound to them, even if there's a curse on the Clan Campbell ever since they murdered the McDonalds in Glencoe. They're names that make you think of mountains, lochs and glens. Battles, blood, adventure. But not Boyle. It sounds like *boil*, they jeer at me in the street sometimes, or at school. Like boiling a kettle, they say. Or even worse, a big boil on the back of your neck.

There's two other John Boyles I know about. There's John Boyle from Castle Street who's some big hard man up the town and leader of his own gang. I've never seen him but everybody's heard of him. Sometimes when I tell people my name they kid on they're dead feart and go, Oho, John Boyle eh? We better watch him, he'll get the Castle Street gang oantae us! The other one is a scruffy boy from Brown's Place that's a bit older than me, another hard nut. Tara, that's his nickname. Tara Boyle. Sounds like Tata Bella that my mammy's always talking about. For the love o' God, she says, comb down your hair and straighten yourself up before ye go out, you'll frighten people, you look like Tata Bella. Tata Bella must be some old tramp or something, I've never seen him. I don't know what Tara means either, though my daddy says it's something to do with the Kings of Ireland. Aye, that'll be right. All I know is, I hate when people call me that nickname – as if I was related to a scruff like Tara Boyle. I don't even like our name anyway.

213

It's my daddy's fault; it's his name.

Toono's got a Scottish name, Brown, and so has Charlie Miller.

It means Ah've goat a clan, Toono says, an' a tartan as well. And so've you, Charlie.

Aye, Ah know, Charlie says, and he looks dead proud. I don't blame him, but I feel jealous all the same.

They both look at me. I don't say anything because what is there to say?

We're back in the close after the parade and we're trying to remember the names of all the Highland Regiments: the Black Watch, the Highland Light Infantry, the Argyll and Sutherland Highlanders, the Gordons . . . We sing the song:

> *A Gordon fur me, a Gordon fur me*
> *If you're no' a Gordon ye're nae use tae me*
> *The Black Watch are braw,*
> *The Seaforths an' a'*
> *But the boanny wee Gordon's the pride o' them a'*

The Seaforth Highlanders! Toono says. We forgoat that yin.

Toono knows all the regiments.

Then he asks me what regiment my daddy was in.

Pioneer Corps, I say, quite proud because I've always liked the name; it reminds me of the US cavalry.

Toono snorts and jeers at me.

The Pioneers? he says. D'ye know whit they wur?

I'm getting worried. I don't like the sound of this.

Naw, I say, but it's a good name intit? It reminds ye—

They used tae dig the graves in the war, Toono says. That's a' they were guid fur. The Pioneers wur a' the

214

mental cases, guys that couldnae read 'n write. Navvies 'n mugs like that. They stuck them a' in the same regiment.

My heart goes like stone, heavy and cold.

My daddy's a navvy, and he can hardly read, though he tries to kid on he can. Toono's daddy's got a trade, and so has Charlie's. I bet they can read no bother, both of them.

If they start jeering at my daddy I'm feart I might burst out greetin'. I've got to get them talking about something else.

But they're no' wan o' the Scoattish regiments, ur they? I ask him.

It's a daft question, but it works.

Och, don't talk daft! Toono jeers. Scoattish regiment ma erse!

But at least it gets him back talking about the Scottish regiments and he starts telling us about this soldier in the Black Watch that won the VC in the war.

I stand there listening but I hardly hear a word he's saying. I'm ashamed, to tell the truth. I'm ashamed of my daddy.

It's a rotten feeling because I love him as well though I could never say that to him or anybody else, naturally, and I get dead embarrassed when he gets all soppy and tries to give me a hug and a kiss, especially if he's drunk. But he's great when he takes me to the football at Love Street or up the racecourse for a kick-about or round to the pond in the Fountain Gardens. You can talk to him then, and he'll tell me stories about himself and his old man back in Donegal and the hard times they had of it after the mammy died and nobody in it but the pair of them and a brokendown old donkey they had about the place, and how glad he was to come over here to Scotland and get work at the totty-howkin'. And that was how he met my mammy, working at the totties, though that's to be a secret between him and me, I'm never to talk about it. For the love a God, he says, never let on to yer mammy Ah tole ye that, she'd go mad altogether, she doesn't like to remember them days. He's great then, when there's just the two of us. And he's a good laugh sometimes when he comes home and tells us about Big Owney or Frank Haggerty and the daft antics they get up to at his work or when he tells his wee jokes about Pat and Mick. But I could never talk to Toono or Charlie about these things, they'd only jeer at me and call me a sissy. Nobody talks like that round here, it's only in books and the pictures you get people talking about stuff like that.

Maybe it's not my daddy's fault he wasn't a kiltie in the Scottish regiments, but I'm ashamed of him just the same.

Mammy, whit did ma daddy dae in the war?

What d'you mean, *ahashki*?

Ah mean, wiz he a sojer, fightin' in the trenches an' that?

Sure how would I know? He doesn't talk about it much . . . They were looking after the Gerry prisoners for a while, I believe. And he was telling me one time they had to bury the dead, God help them. Can ye imagine? A terrible job that must be, the Lord bless us and save us . . . The craitchurs, ye'd feel sorry for them.

So now I know. Toono was right.

My daddy's always getting me embarrassed these

days. You're supposed to look up to your father, but how can I? I want him to be like Flash Gordon or Johnny Weissmuller, or even Father Murphy or Big Bill Campbell, but not a hope. He's just plain Mick Boyle. He can't help it, I suppose.

Still, I'm going to stop calling him my daddy. It sounds a bit sissy anyway.

Ma aul' man: that's what Toono calls his.

I used to think I would never say that. It sounds as if you don't even like him, he's nothing to do with you.

That's what I'm calling him from now on.

Me and my daddy and my Uncle John and Old Jimmy Bradley are in Bishopton for the day with Auntie Bradley because she's visiting her sister Sadie. But as soon as we get off the train my Uncle John says he could fair go a whisky so he takes us all into this hotel lounge near the station. And in there my Auntie Bradley meets a woman she knows from Donegal, a Mrs McClardie, who starts telling us a story about a neighbour of hers.

Oh, she's a proper madam, that one, says Mrs McClardie. Ah remember wan day we were all sitting in a lounge bar and when my man God rest his soul asked us What'll ye have to drink? every last wan of us ordered a pale ale. But not herself, ah no, not a bit of it. I'll have an Export, says Lady Muck. A pale ale wasn't good enough for her, she had to have an Export.

For the life of me I can't see what's so bad about asking for an Export, but all the grownups look very shocked and start shaking their heads and tut-tutting, so I suppose it must be pretty bad right enough.

But it's not half as bad as what happens later on,

217

when we're round at Sadie's having tea and sandwiches. We're all sitting there sipping our tea though we can't settle down properly because Sadie keeps mooching about the place as if she's looking for something. She's a very old whitehaired woman, much older than Auntie Bradley, and she'll get up suddenly and start looking behind the cushions and keeking under the couch and under the chairs. We're all sitting there watching her and looking at each other, wondering what she's up to.

For the luvva Gawd, Sadie, says Auntie Bradley, would ye sit yerself down, or what's the matter wit' ye at all?

Ah don't mind me, says Sadie. It's jist a wee thing Ah'm doin' for meself.

Have ye lost somethin', or what is it?

Ah haven't we all lost somethin', says Sadie, Every last wan o' us.

She lets out a big sigh.

But pay no heed to me, don't worry yer heads about it. It's oney a wee thing.

Oney, she says. Like my daddy.

She sits back down and we're none the wiser.

My Auntie Bradley waits till her back's turned then makes a face to the rest of us as much as to say her sister's away with the fairies.

I don't think that's fair. Sadie's been nice to us, even if she acts a bit odd.

But that's not the bad thing.

After a while Sadie settles down and Auntie Bradley starts blethering away to her. She seems to do all the talking nowadays because Old Jimmy Bradley's been feeling poorly and hardly ever says a word. It's a pity, I miss the ghost stories he used to tell us.

That oul' bitch Bridie McClardie was there, yapping out of her as usual, Auntie Bradley is saying, and d'ye know, when John here got up to buy a round and asked us all what we wanted, would you believe this, she asked for an Export! I'll have an Export, says her ladyship, as nice as ninepence. Would ye be up to her? The rest o' us were happy enough drinking pale ale but d'ye think that was good enough for her? Ah no, not a bit of it. It had to be an Export. Oh aye, she's a proper madam, that one.

I look at my daddy and I'm thinking, my Auntie Bradley's the one that's away with the fairies, she's got it all mixed up, surely he'll say something? Old Jimmy and my Uncle John don't say anything; fair enough, I suppose, they're her family, they have to stick up for her. But no, my old man's just as bad. The three of them just sit there shaking their heads and tut-tutting all over again, the way they did in the lounge bar, and I'm shocked to see how a person can steal somebody else's story and sit there telling a barefaced lie and get away with it when there's people there who should know it's not true.

I'm Top Boy in the class and Rosemary McKim is Top Girl. She probably scored higher than me in the exam because she's dead clever but we don't ask, so we can say we're even. At the prizegiving we sit together at the front of the Assembly. She's a nicelooking lassie and she keeps smiling at me with her rosy lips and I wonder if maybe she could be my girlfriend. Top Boy and Top Girl, we'd be a good match.

When I'm called up to the platform I get First Prize, a big heavy book with hundreds of pages. It's *David Copperfield* by Charles Dickens. Pat Foley's the

Second Boy and he gets a book called *Children of the New Forest*.

Afterwards when we're comparing books his looks much nicer. It's got a great colour picture on the cover, a boy and girl lost in a dark, mysterious forest that reminds me of Grimms Fairy Tales. Mine's only got old-fashioned printing on the cover.

I ask him if he wants to swap.

You can see he likes the idea of getting the First Prize book, but he's not that sure.

D'ye mean it? he says.

Aye, I say, though I'm not too sure myself.

But it turns out there are wee labels inside printed with our names and saying what prizes we got, so we think maybe we better not. Mine says:

Awarded to JOHN BOYLE
First (Boys) in School Examinations

Then the date. Afterwards I'm glad I never swapped because *David Copperfield* turns out to be a great story once you get into it and anyway I'd have got a terrible row from my mammy. My old man's dead proud especially when he's got a drink in him and he makes me show the book to all our visitors and they all say, Good on ye, John. Especially my Uncle John. He asks to see the book every time he comes round, and sits there holding it in his big hands and looking at the label inside as if he can hardly believe it.

David Ka-Copperfield, by Chacha-Charles Dickens, eh? he says. That's grand. D'ye know, Ah've always wanted tae read that. D'ye think Ah could ga-get the len' o' it when ye've fafa-finished?

Oh aye, sure, I tell him, dead proud that my uncle wants to borrow my book.

I'm that proud I even hurry up and finish it so I can lend it to him. I'm showing off a bit as well, to tell the truth, so he can see what a fast reader I am.

My mammy's not too pleased.

Well I hope to God he brings it back, is all I can say. That's a valuable book, ye know.

I'm puzzled. Why would he not bring it back?

Ah now, she says. People can be funny sometimes. I'll say no more than that.

That's the trouble with my mammy. Never trusts anybody.

The teachers at school and the priests at Mass are always telling us about the soul. Everybody's got a soul and it's immortal, it's the part of us that carries on living after we're dead, when we go to Heaven or Hell or Purgatory. But the big mystery is, nobody knows where it is. We know where the brain is, and where the heart is, but when we ask the teachers where the soul is all they can say is, It's a Mystery, and look mysterious when they're saying it. But it seems to me if the soul exists it must be somewhere, even though we can't see it, like America before Christopher Columbus discovered it.

Round about this time I'm getting worried about my wullie, because it's always sticking up when I wake up in the morning and then it gets hard again when I'm sitting upstairs on the bus going to school, and I have to hold my haversack over it when I get off so nobody'll see. Sometimes when I'm out in the lavvy with the door snibbed I look at it, and especially the wee hairs that have started growing there, because that's another thing I'm worried about. I'm sitting on the pan one day feeling about down there even though you're not supposed to because it's a sin but I keep at it anyway and suddenly I feel this big lump in a wee kinda bag behind my wullie. And I'm dead feart, thinking maybe I'm deformed or I've got some terrible disease. I've never heard any of my pals saying anything about a lump down there, though some boys are always talking about their wullies, especially Toono and James McGovern.

And that's when the idea comes to me that maybe I've discovered the soul. This comes as a big relief to me and it's dead exciting as well. It makes sense the more you think about it, because if everybody keeps telling us we've got a soul, how come nobody can tell us where it is? I must admit it's very odd that nobody's ever discovered the soul before me, but then I think maybe nobody but me has ever touched themselves down there, it's such a terrible sin, or if they have they're too ashamed to admit it. Or maybe it means I'm different, unique, picked out by Our Lord to make this great discovery. I'm dead excited because I know that even if a discovery is just an accident, like James Watt discovering steam power by watching the lid bouncing up and down on a pot, it still counts. And I think to myself maybe I'll be famous – The Boy Who Discovered the Soul. Like The Boy Who Saved Holland, putting his finger in the dyke.

But when I start really feeling about down there I find there's two lumps, not just the one, and this gets me worried all over again. Nobody ever said anything about us having two souls. Unless maybe I'm the only person in the world who has. But then I remember about the Holy Trinity, which it says in the catechism is the mystery of Three Persons in One God, so I think maybe the soul could be something the same.

Anyway this is my big secret for a while because I'm too shy and feart to talk to anybody about it. But then I think I might have to tell it in confession because sometimes when I'm fiddling about down there it makes my wullie hard, and even though it's in a good cause, the discovery of the soul, I'm worried in case I might be in a State of Sin. So I go up to St Mary's because I'm an altarboy at St James's and I'm feart Father Murphy will know my voice.

I pick out a priest's name that I've never heard of and go into his confessional box. I start by telling him the wee sins, the venial sins, then I get to the main subject.

Please, Father, Ah think I've committed the sin of impurity.

Ye think, he says. He's Scottish, by the sound of him.

Well now. So tell me, son, was it in thought word or deed?

In deed, Father, I say. Ah don't think it was a real sin, though, because there was a good reason for it.

Oh aye? he says. And what good reason could there possibly be for the sin of impurity?

So I take a deep breath and tell him the whole story, about how I think I might've discovered the soul.

He doesn't say anything for a long time then I hear these wee choking noises like somebody in church trying hard not to cough. Holy Mother o' God, I hear him whispering, and at first I think he's praying to Our Lady for the redemption of my immortal soul then I realize he's just muttering away to himself in there. May God forgive us, he's saying, for keeping these innocents in a state of ignorance. Then he says something else, something about Our chickens coming home to roost and As ye sow, so shall ye reap, but none of this makes any sense to me so I don't say anything. At last he clears his throat and asks me my age. Eleven, Father, I tell him, an' a half. Well, son, he says, What you've told me about is nothing to do with the soul, believe me. It's just normal physical development in a boy of your age. Nothing to worry about, nothing at all. Did your parents no' tell you yet about the birds and the bees?

No Father, I say, and I'm dead embarrassed because I've got an idea the birds and the bees is something to do with men and women and making babies.

Well, he says, this is not a subject for the confessional, son, but just ask your father or your mother to explain to you about the birds and the bees and with the help of God it'll all start to make sense. Now say three Hail Marys for your penance like a good boy and go in peace.

I'm dead disappointed that I haven't discovered the soul after all, and I'm not going to be famous, though I have to admit it's a big relief that I'm not sick or deformed either, and I'm thinking Thank God I never told this story to any of my pals because I'd never've heard the last of it. But the birds and the bees will have to wait, because nobody in our house ever talks about things like that. It'll just have to stay a mystery, like where the soul is.

I'm to go out to Ferguslie Park to visit the Bradleys because Old Jimmy is very poorly these days.

God help him, says my mammy, I doubt he's not long for this world.

My old man's supposed to come with me but he's not back yet from his work so I have to go on my own.

Overtime, supposed to be, says my mammy. Believe it if you like.

She's fed up because she thinks he's in the pub for a pint.

When I get to the Bradleys I'm shocked at the change in Old Jimmy. He's an old man, but I always thought he was quite handsome, with his cropped grey hair and his strong jaw blue from shaving. I used to love to watch him sitting by the fire telling his yarns, lighting his pipe with the wee spills he makes himself and keeps in a jar near the grate. He makes them with the greasy paper you get on sliced loaves, because it's easy to light. He tears the paper in lengths then folds and twists it tight till the spill is straight and stiff. He does it slow and steady, the way he does most things, and he makes it look easy. But it's not. Many's the time he's let me try and mine always come out floppy.

Auntie Bradley's in the kitchen making the tea, so I sit on the couch watching Old Jimmy in his armchair, staring into the fire puffing at his pipe as usual. Except the pipe's not lit and he doesn't seem to care. There are no spills in the jar either and the fire's nearly gone out, just a few red embers glowing in the ashes.

What shocks me is his face. It's collapsed. The strong jaw has caved in and his mouth is shrunk tight and wrinkled because he hasn't got his teeth in. His face is that thin and wee it makes his eyes look huge.

Like Speed that day, drowning in the rockpool.

Auntie Bradley sticks her head in.

We have no sugar, she says. Ah'll just go down and borry some from Mrs Toner below. Ah'll no be long.

You can sit there, you'll be gran' company for poor Jimmy.

When she shuts the door behind her I feel awkward. I try to get him talking, thinking maybe he'll tell me some of the old stories and that'll cheer him up. But he only sits and nods and stares into the ashes, and after a while I give up.

We're just sitting there. All I can hear is the old clock on the mantelpiece ticking, and the sucking of Old Jimmy's pipe and him breathing heavy through his nose.

From time to time his foot gives a twitch.

Suddenly the clock whirs and chimes. The noise makes me jump in my chair.

Old Jimmy turns his head. He looks at me as if he's just noticed me.

Who're you? he says.

He sounds wary. Suspicious.

I try to laugh but it comes out half choked.

It's OK Uncle Jimmy. It's only me.

Aye, but who *are* ye? he says again.

I'm worried but I try to sound calm.

Ah'm John. Ye know, John Boyle. Uncle John's nephew. Big John, yer son, he's my uncle. Remember?

He's still staring at me. He doesn't know me from Adam. Then his eyes shift to something behind me. He looks scared.

Who's he that fella?

I turn around. There's nothing there but a standard lamp with a fringe on the shade.

Naebody there, Uncle Jimmy. Only me. John.

He's still staring back there. Now he's making me feart.

226

Ah don't mind you, he says. You look all right. But I don't like the look of yon fella ye brought along wit' ye.

I swivel round again. I swear to God I'm half expecting to see a ghost. Or the banshee, God forbid.

But there's nothing.

When I turn back to Old Jimmy he's trying to stand up, shaking on his feet, leaning on the arm of his chair. He points at the thing behind me.

Ah don't like the look o' yon fella at all. Not wan bit. Who brought him here? Don't let that fella come anear me.

He looks terrified. You'd swear he was staring at somebody standing in the corner.

I wish to God my daddy was here. I wish I wasn't here.

I don't know what to do.

The front door opens. My Auntie Bradley's back.

My mammy keeps dropping hints to Uncle John about my *David Copperfield.* That's months he's had it now.

The first few times he says he's still reading it, it's an awful long book. Then he starts saying he can't find it.

But da-don't you wawa-worry, he says, I have it in the house somewhere. Oh, I'll ba-bring it back all right, nana-never fear.

She just smiles and kids him on about it but it's a different story after he's gone.

Would ye be up to that big man? she says to me. I swear to God, he's trying to steal that book from you.

Aw come on, Mammy, I jeer at her. Whit wid he dae that fur? Anyway, it's goat ma name printed on the label.

Indeed it has, she says. And isn't he John Boyle as well as yourself?

I can hardly believe what she's saying.

Och, ma Uncle John wid never dae a thing like that. How come ye always think bad about people?

She stands there shaking her head.

I'm only speaking the truth, she says. That's the way of the world, I'm afraid.

I don't want to believe her.

Anyway, I say, even if he did try somethin' like that, it wid never work, it's goat the date oan the label.

She gives me her sideyways look, the one that says, You might think you know it all but you know nothing.

Dates can be changed, she says. Between your Uncle John and your daddy, I doubt there's a pair o' them in it.

Old Jimmy Bradley's dead.

When we hear the news my mammy sends me up to Auntie Bradley's to pay my respects. I don't really want to go to a sad empty house where somebody's died, but when I get there it's not like that at all, there's a crowd of grownups in the living room drinking and talking in low voices and I don't know what to do with myself. So I go into the kitchen because my Auntie Bradley's in there rinsing glasses and I say what I've been practising all the way on the bus.

Auntie Bradley, Ah wis dead sorry tae hear about Uncle Jimmy and ma mammy says Ah wis I was tae pay ma respects.

Ah God love ye, it's a sad time for us all right but I'm glad you could come anyway, says Auntie Bradley. Poor Jimmy, she sighs, God rest him. Ah well, I suppose it was for the best, he was awful bad there in the finish-up.

She dries her hands and looks at me.

Would ye like to see him?

I'm horrified; I don't know what to say. I had no idea Old Jimmy's dead body would still be in the house, I thought it would be away in the church or somewhere by now.

Come on and I'll show ye, she says.

She takes me into a room I've never been in before, and there's a big polished coffin with brass handles on a kind of table in the middle and inside it is Old Jimmy.

We stand there beside it. I don't want to look at him. There's a clock ticking somewhere behind us. A bus goes by outside, on the far side of the road. I can hear my Auntie Bradley breathing. I can smell her snuff smell.

Doesn't he look lovely? she whispers.

I'm feart to look but I have to.

Aye, I whisper back.

It's true enough: Old Jimmy's face looks handsome again with the blue jaw filled out and strong.

Ah'll have to go back in now, Auntie Bradley says, but ye can stan' here a while an' say a wee prayer for him.

And away she goes and leaves me there by the coffin.

I'm feart at first in there by myself with a dead man but after a while it's OK. I just keep looking in at Old Jimmy, at his irongrey hair neat and combed and his face peaceful and holylooking with his eyes closed. His skin is not saggy any more, it's been smoothed firm over his brow and nose and chin, and it's a bluey-white waxy colour you can nearly see through, like marble. Like the statue of a saint.

I stand there for a while trying to think of a prayer but nothing comes; I'm not in the right mood. I'm looking at Old Jimmy's blue jaw and thinking, He must've died with his teeth in.

Like in the cowboy pictures: He Died With His Boots On.

I nearly burst out laughing and I'm mortified because I'm supposed to be sad but it's like when you get the giggles at Mass, you can't help it. I should be saying a prayer but maybe it doesn't matter; for all I know Old Jimmy might be in Heaven already and at peace, because he looks a lot better dead than the last time I saw him alive.

We're flittin'. My mammy's got us a new house in Ferguslie Park so we're leaving 4 Galloway Street at last. Barney Molloy has got us the loan of a lorry and he's up and down the stairs with my old man all day long humping furniture and loading it on the back. Sometimes they get stuck on the corner of the landing and we'll hear the cursing and banging echoing up the stairs.

Steady on there now, Mick, says Barney. Steady now.

Noises of wood creaking and squealing. Then my old man:

Arra the curse o' Christ on it!

Jesus Mary and Joseph, says my mammy. They'll have my few bits of furniture smashed to smithereens.

She's up in our house with me and my wee brothers and sisters and we're all helping though she says we're just getting in the way.

I'm up to a hundred at ye, she keeps saying. Up to High Doh is what I am.

But we can see she's pleased to be getting out of Galloway Street at last, where me and Frankie and Vincent have to sleep three to a bed in the big room with Margaret in the spare bed and herself and my old man and wee Bernard and baby Irene all cramped together in the kitchen. She wanted Gallowhill or Hunterhill because you get A Better Class of People there, but at least Ferguslie Park will be nicer than this dump.

The Lord save us, she says. How could it be any worse?

I don't tell her what Toono said when I told him.

Feegie? Fuck. Yeez better watch yersels there. Feegie's dead rough.

Feegie, he calls it. Some people even call it the Jungle. That's another thing I don't tell her.

At first I'm worried. Toono's dead rough himself; if he thinks it's rough, it must be *really* rough. But then I think maybe he's just jealous, getting left behind.

Ferguslie Park. You've got to admit it's got a nice sound to it. Better than Galloway Street anyway.

It's a big housing scheme outside the town and the houses there are very well built, they say. Ours has got an inside lavvy and a bath and a front garden with a hedge and I'm getting a whole room to myself so I'm happy.

When the lorry's nearly loaded the taxi comes to pick up my mammy and the weans and take them to our new house. Some wee weans from down the end of the street come and stand beside me on the pavement because when they see the taxi they think it's a wedding and they'll get the pennies flung out the window. When the taxi pulls away from the kerb and there's no pennies they look scunnered.

It's no' a weddin', I say to them. Jist a flittin'.

I don't want them thinking we're stingy.

They just give me a dirty look and wander away.

Because I'm the eldest I'm allowed to stay behind and go on the lorry with my old man and Barney Molloy. My old man can't drive but Barney can so they're in the cab and I'm to sit on the back in a space they've left for me between the sideboard and the back of the armchair.

Before we leave we go up to check the house is empty and I stand for a while in my favourite place at the sink, looking out the window. I stroke my hand along the copper tap that's like a swan's neck and I'm sad because it's the last time. I always liked that tap, it was a good pal to me.

It's an open lorry so they've got the furniture covered with old Army blankets and tied down under a tarpaulin in case it rains and I'm cosy there in my wee hideyhole. I'm holding my cricket bat I got for Christmas so I could be like Harry Wharton at Greyfriars School but I never got much chance because hardly anybody in Galloway Street plays cricket and nobody's even heard of Harry Wharton.

The lorry pulls away from the close and it's a covered wagon heading across the prairie to the wild frontier with me riding shotgun with my cricket bat. It's Injun country out there, but there's no cavalry escort any more; the Pioneer Corps got wiped out by the Apaches. No survivors. It's up to me, I'm the man of the house now. I put my rifle to my shoulder and sight along it, scanning the horizon for Injuns. I aim up at our two windows at the top of number four, looking

232

bare and empty now without the curtains. Then the sights on my Winchester travel down the old tenement's sooty face past the Deveneys' house, past number six where the McNultys used to live and along to number eight where Charlie lived. They've all left already, moved away to the schemes. Except the Deveneys; they went to Australia.

> And to Australia's sunny shore
> He was inclined to roam.

I try to picture my old pal Wullie growing up like Jack Duggan, the wild colonial boy:

> He robbed the rich, he helped the poor
> He stabbed James MacAvoy
> A terror to Australia was
> The wild colonial boy

I can't see it. Toono, maybe. But not Wullie.

Just before the wagon turns the corner at Galbraith's, I aim a shot at the railway wall at the bottom of the street where Wee Joe Kerr got crushed to death and the long goods trains used to clank past at all hours and make the houses shudder and the long lonely whistle would wake me up feeling lost and feart in the dark.

The wagon heads up Underwood Road towards the gasworks and our new life in Ferguslie Park and I take a few last potshots in case there's any renegades or snipers still holed up behind the boarded window-holes in Brown's Place. *Widden windies*, Toono calls them. It'll all be knocked down soon, they say. The swingpark where Mister Deveney fought the Bluenose and Wullie smashed my finger is nothing but a twisted wreck now and all the tenements are deserted, like a ghost town. It's hard to imagine Galloway Street could ever go the same way.

But that's what Barney Molloy says.

Ah it will, he says, it will surely. Them days are done.

Afterword

1993

When I last said goodbye to Aunt Mary at the cottage on Achill Island, I took away with me a bag of Flahavan's oats. On the mountain road above, my mother and Aunt Annie were waiting in the car for me to drive them to Dublin for their flight back to Glasgow. Mary was 'convalescing' at home after major surgery for breast cancer long neglected and, though none of us voiced the thought, we knew in our hearts that we might never see her again. But there it was. It was the end of our visit and we had to get back to our own lives.

I had bought a stock of provisions at the store in the Sound to make sure Mary had enough to last her until September, when she would be taken into care by the nuns at Keel. I threw in the bag of oats on impulse, to replace those I had consumed with such relish during the visit, having rediscovered my taste for porridge. As I was leaving she pressed the bag into my hands.

'Haven't I bags full of them yet in that box in the kitchen? I have enough there to last me a lifetime,' she said without irony. 'Take it with you.'

'A souvenir, you mean?' I said, teasing her.

'Oh yes,' she said merrily, and using her stick for support lowered herself carefully onto the rickety settee, dismissing me. 'A souvenir! That's a good one, eh, Rocky?'

Rocky, her squat little mongrel, was perched in his usual His Master's Voice pose in the dusty armchair on the other side of the hearth. That was my last sight of them, the old spinster and her dog sharing the joke across the smouldering turf fire, Mary giggling gummily behind her fist like a little girl caught out in some mischief.

Back home in Brussels, my wife and daughter showed little enthusiasm for porridge, though wee Sean, bless his heart, would take the odd bowl to show solidarity with his dad. Now and again I would make up a bowl for myself, usually early on Sunday mornings before Sally and the kids came down. As I drowsily measured out my cupful of oats in our warm, humming kitchen, my thoughts would drift to the old woman living out her death sentence on the bleak Atlantic shore. When the bag was nearly empty I kept it in the cupboard, loath somehow to throw it away. As if it were indeed a souvenir.

The week before Christmas came the news of Mary's death. The nuns' home at Keel was closing for the Christmas holiday and she had had to be transferred by ambulance back to the Sacred Heart home in Castlebar, a place she hated, as I had reason to know. She had died there the following day.

A few days later my sister Margaret and I were sitting in the little office at the back of Lavelle's General Store in Achill Sound. We looked around at the chipboard desk on trestles with its spiked bills and papers, the old-fashioned black telephone, the pile of well-thumbed order books with ancient carbon paper fringing the leaves, the few dusty buff folders on rickety wood shelves.

'This is where it all happens,' I said. 'We're in the Nerve Centre here.'

My sarcasm was misplaced. Mick Lavelle had turned out to be not only the proprietor of the general store, but the town's undertaker as well. And we had just learned from his brother, John Lavelle, the solicitor, the name of the sole beneficiary of Mary's will.

'Berry. Irene Berry,' he said. 'Does the name mean anything to you?'

Irene was our youngest sister, who had been unable to make the trip. This was a shock: everybody had expected the place to go to Aunt Annie.

'You can see how it will be difficult to break this to Mrs Millar,' the solicitor said.

When he'd gone, Margaret and I sat for a while in silence. Then Margaret started to laugh.

'That's Mary all over,' she said. 'Awkward to the last.'

Mary, Mary, quite contrary. I could imagine her having a good cackle at us all. I remembered the first time I'd come back to Achill to see her, the time I'd brought Sally and our first-born, Stephanie. We'd left the baby sleeping in the car parked on the rough road above the cottage, which looked dilapidated and abandoned, and were making our way gingerly down the rutted, stony path when a stout little mongrel rushed out of the overgrown grass and started barking and skipping around us. We stopped, wary of a strange dog, then a figure appeared at the corner of the house, a tall old woman in garish cast-offs and heavy boots. For a moment I feared we'd disturbed squatting tinkers, then, 'Come back here, Rocky, good boy,' the woman called and I knew it was Mary, recognized her after nearly thirty years.

She'd let on not to know me at first, squinting at me suspiciously when I told her who I was. I had to remind her that I'd been here with her as a boy, had even gone to the local school. To my surprise I could recall the names of some of my classmates from that distant time: Brian Masterson, Paddy Ann, Annie Harry . . . But it wasn't until I mentioned Mary's own Aunt Bridget that I got a response.

'Begod, d'ye remember the Yank? She's dead now these twenty-five years, God rest her . . . Ah well, I suppose it must be you, right enough.' She looked at me closely. 'But you've changed, you've changed. And is this your wife?'

'Yes, this is Sally,' I said, relieved that the focus of her scrutiny had moved on. 'She's American, too.'

'Is she, by God? Another Yankee Doodle?' said merry Mary. 'Hello, Sally. Ye're welcome, dear. By God,' she said to me, 'Isn't she the lovely girl altogether?'

'Oh no,' Sally laughed, shaking hands with her. 'The lovely girl is our little one, Stephanie. She's up there sleeping in the car.'

'Jaipers, is that right? Well, maybe it's the best place for her. God knows it's a rough sort of a place here to be bringing a child. Dog rough we are here, *ahashki*. Dog rough in Boston, as the one said. Sit down, Rocky!' she said to the little dog who was still panting around our legs. 'He's a grand dog, God love him, but he's all excited.'

'Rocky? What kind of name's that for a dog, Mary?' I asked, starting to relax now, teasing her.

'Rocky Marciano!' said Mary, with an explosive giggle, shielding her toothless mouth with her fist. 'Did ye never hear of the boxer, Rocky Marciano? The champ?'

And here the old woman hunched into a fighter's defensive crouch and began jabbing and feinting and skipping about on the rough ground in front of the cottage with her little dog yapping around her in the dust.

'Would he not put you in mind of him?' she cried, 'with the little patcheen on his eye, and the cute sort of a way he has about him, isn't he a dead ringer for Rocky Marciano?'

When we got back, there was not much time left to get ready for the funeral Mass. I put on the dark grey shirt and black and grey silk tie I had brought to wear with my charcoal suit and heavy overcoat. Not having been to Mass for years, I was enjoying the ritual of dressing up for this one. Then I went down to the cottage. I was still uneasy about the will — the bombshell in store for Aunt Annie and her family was preying on my mind — but in the last-minute rush to get ready no awkward questions were asked.

In an unexpected lull while the others had gone to a neighbour's house I found myself alone in the kitchen. Gingerly, being careful of my clothes, I banked some turf on the fire with the tongs and looked around. No, nothing much had changed. Years ago, Aunt Mary had had someone fix cheap plywood cladding — 'beauty boards' she called them — on the walls to keep the damp at bay. But I could remember the original walls

239

from a time long ago, the time I had first come over here with her.

To get to the cottage we had had to wade through wet grass and weeds that came up to my chest. Then when Aunt Mary turned the big iron key in the lock, the door would not open: the wood had warped and jammed fast in its frame. Aunt Mary, a big strapping woman at that time, put her shoulder to it and pushed hard, cursing it. With a loud crack it flew open. Big slabs of plaster dropped from the walls and ceiling, adding to the rubble on the stone floor. The air inside was heavy with dust and damp and decay. Seeing a small colourful object just inside the doorway, I picked it up. It was a picture of the Sacred Heart of Jesus, still nailed to its bit of plaster, its glass cracked, its frame broken. The image showed the Lord Jesus, wearing his crown of thorns, pulling his robe aside to reveal his Sacred Heart, which was ringed with fire. The legend read: 'I will protect the house in which the picture of my Sacred Heart is exposed and honoured.' I smiled at the irony and pointed it out to Aunt Mary, thinking to cheer her up. But she only scolded me for daring to make a joke of the Sacred Heart and I was sad. Some days later she placed a little framed snapshot of me on the dresser, saying: 'You're the man of the house now, Johnny. You're the one has to look after us.' I felt overwhelmed at the huge responsibility I was taking over from the Sacred Heart but dared not say so. Many years later I learned that Aunt Mary had tried to keep me in Ireland, even tried to adopt me: my mother had had 'the divil of a job' to get me back.

When I had first come back to Achill as a grown

man, I was amazed to see that the photograph still stood on the dresser. Now, as I reminisced by the fireside, I could hear Aunt Annie mooching about in Aunt Mary's old room.

'Annie?' I called in to her. 'D'you remember that wee photo of me Mary used to keep on the dresser? It's not in there by any chance, is it?'

'Aye, I believe it is. Come in, come in. Is this the one you mean?'

Annie was standing by the dressing table in the musty bedroom smoothing on her gloves and looking down at the little black and white snapshot in its cheap bakelite frame.

'By jingo, that's an old one, right enough,' she said, moving away to the bed, rummaging for something in her handbag.

'Forty years, near enough,' I said. I picked it up and looked at it, rubbing away the grime from the glass with my thumb. I saw a cheekyfaced boy of about nine, wearing what looked like an army jerkin and standing against a dark tenement wall. And forty years fell away.

I'm in the kitchen in Sraheens, on my stool by the fire. Auntie Mary's in her armchair and the Yank's standing at the rickety table reading my school report out loud to us in her Yankee twang.

Top of the clay-ass for English grammar and composition. By Gally, ye'll make an ace reporter one day. We'll be proud of ye yet.

Ah we will, says Auntie Mary, we will surely. Isn't Mickey Tom always praising him? He says Johnny does be making up little stories to tell him when they're down at the fishing in the stream below. He's that old-fashioned, he has poor Mickey Tom half-kilt laughing at him.

I squat on my hunkers on the riverbank watching Mickey Tom jiggling the rod in the rock pool.

D'ye think ye'll stay here and be a fisherman, Mickey Tom?

Ah God love ye, no, he says. Sure what would I be doing in a place like this? No fear. No flies on me, boy. I'll be away to Ameriky soon with God's help, and I'll have a big public house in Boston or Chigago, maybe, and you can come over and see me when you're a bigshot making pots o' money and we'll have a drink to the good old days fishing in Shraheens.

Fishin', eh? Staunin' here freezin', ye mean, catchin' nuthin' but the cauld?

Ah Jaisus, Johnny, will ye shtop? Ye'd make the cat laugh, so ye would.

My nine-year-old self grinned out at me from the frame with a kind of cocky defiance, all his dreams intact. Glancing up at the canted, cracked mirror above the dressing table, I met the troubled gaze of an over-dressed middle-aged man. No ace reporter he. The only writing he did nowadays was advertising copy, speeches, translations. The only stories he told were jokes and anecdotes, endlessly recycled and embroidered in the telling. Not to mention his main source of income, the voiceovers for TV commercials and corporate videos. His talent was a superficial gravitas, fake sincerity deployed to sell things he neither knew nor cared about. I'm a fully paid-up member of the bullshit brigade, he would breezily explain. As if owning up to it made it somehow less bad. Look how clear-eyed I am, was his message to the world. No self-delusion there. Jesus.

> *Then wear the gold hat, if that will please her*
> *If you can bounce high, bounce for her too.*
> *Till she cry 'Lover,*
> *Gold-hatted, high-bouncing lover,*
> *I must have you!'*

The lines of verse that preface *The Great Gatsby* echoed in my mind, conjuring images: a jester on the high wire, capering above the void; a fan-dance of masks.

The man in the mirror had been wearing the gold hat, the shifting masks, all his adult life.

Who had he been trying to please?

Or to kid.

I felt Annie's curious gaze on me and looked up at her.

'Would you mind if I took this?'

'What? Aye, surely,' she said. 'Why wouldn't you? It's yours after all.'

I slid the photograph into my overcoat pocket.

'A souvenir,' I said.

Margaret and I were the first to arrive at the church, which was empty save for a few old women huddled in black shawls near the back. I did not know the faces but felt somehow that I should and so nodded gravely to them as I strode up the aisle. The simple wood coffin was placed just below the altar, a tall candle burning at its head: a substantial wreath and various Mass cards

243

had been placed on the lid. Margaret made a space there for our own flowers and looked through the Mass cards, reading out the names in an undertone. The names sounded familiar but I could put faces to none of them.

A young priest now appeared and invited us into the vestry. He suggested that as members of the immediate family we might like to read part of the service and gave us a few minutes to look over two passages he had marked for us.

When we came back out into the chapel, the Scottish contingent were settling in the first two pews. Other groups of people were dotted around the well of the church. A tall, serene nun in a white hood glided up the aisle and shook hands graciously with Annie, then with Margaret and me. She was the Sister from the convent hospital at Keel.

'Ah, poor Mary,' she said. 'We would never have sent her from us if we had known she was so close to her time. May she rest in peace.'

Other mourners followed, all strangers to me, though something in the broad, big-boned faces caused me to look closely at them. 'Poor Mary, God rest her,' and 'Sorry for your trouble,' they murmured, shaking hands, and went back to their seats.

Standing at the lectern, I decided to give a subdued reading with just an undercurrent of emotion, using my everyday, not my professional voice. At the same time I despaired of myself for being so calculating at such a moment. When I started reading, the unthinkable happened: to my chagrin I faltered, unsure what my true voice was.

Mick Lavelle in his undertaker role supervised the bearing of the coffin from the church. My brother

Frank and I were at the head, the Mullens and the Millars at the waist and feet. With the help of Lavelle and a flushed youth who helped out in his shop, we hoisted the coffin onto our shoulders and all six of us – Ah, Mary, I thought, you lived your life apart from men and you have them all around you when you're dead – moved in slow, shuffling procession down the aisle.

After another flurry of condolences outside the church, the cortège got under way. Lavelle had told us not to expect many cars, but in my wing mirror I counted at least ten behind us. Who were all these people? Where had they come from? Why did so many of them look familiar? I reflected that for all Mary's contrariness, which at one time or another had alienated everyone around her, the little community was doing her proud: a life was a life; its passing had to be honoured.

The hearse moved slowly out of the Sound and the cortège wound along a route that I had once walked, that longago summer, to school: it was called the Bog Road then, a rough lane fringed with singing hedgerows in which I and my pal Brian Masterson once found and kept secret from our schoolmates, who would have plundered it, a bird's nest with three burnished, speckled eggs. Now the road was smoothly tarmacked, bordered by the groomed lawns of expensive bungalows and renamed the Atlantic Drive, and Brian Masterson had died years ago of heart failure in Pittsburg.

At the cemetery, when we had again solemnly shouldered the coffin, I had a perverse urge to laugh at the thought of the picture we must make: an absurd, monstrous duodecipede groping its way down the sloping path inside the gate. But on the first weathered gravestone that we passed I read:

IN LOVING MEMORY
OF
MARY SWEENEY

and I was sobered. Another Mary Sweeney, another circle closed.

Two men in cloth caps were stooped by the mounds of fresh earth that marked the graveside, placing rough wood supports across the deep, narrow gap. As the coffin approached they pulled off their caps and helped guide it onto the struts, then stood with bowed heads to one side, hands crossed in front of them. I looked at them and gave each a nod of recognition. The first was Big Liam the handyman, a 'fine-lookin' fella' in Mary's own words and one of the few tradesmen she trusted to do the odd repair around the cottage that she could bring herself to pay for. The other man tapped a finger to his forehead in a queer kind of ducking motion that was part greeting, part obeisance, and with a pang I recognized Mickey Lynch. 'Ah, poor Mickey Tom, he's destroyed with the drink,' Mary had told me when I had last asked about him. Mickey Tom had never left Achill. Where now, I wondered, were his dreams of the pub in America? Yet in this beaten man I could still see the young Mickey Tom who used to take me fishing in the stream below the big house where he lived with his widowed mother, Mary Tom. And now I recognized the name on the headstone of the neighbouring grave: Mary Lynch, *née* Cooney – the same Mary Tom who had been a mother to me too that summer, and always had a smile and a sandwich and a glass of milk for me, since there was small chance, she would say without malice, that I was being looked after properly at Aunt Mary's. Mary Tom had felt sorry for me since the day, not long after we arrived, when Aunt Mary sent me over to her house to ask a favour.

Ah cannae do that, I'm saying to Auntie Mary, nearly greetin' with the shame of it. Ah'd be mortified!

Ah, go on wit' ye. Have a bit of gumption, will ye? Just tell her your daddy's coming over from Scotland to visit us and could she spare us a chicken so we'll have something dacent to offer him for his dinner. Sure she'll never miss it! Isn't she well off, over there in her big house?

Mary Tom opens her door and I'm standing there struck dumb with shame.

What is it, ahashki? Come in, come in, she says, and when she finally gets it out of me looks hard at me to make sure I'm not kidding her on then throws back her head and starts laughing.

By God, that's Mary all over. You couldn't bate Mary, ahashki. You couldn't bate her with a shtick.

She takes me out to the yard and I stand there surrounded by squawking hens as she corners and catches one then shows me how to hold it because City shlickers like yourself, she says, are not used to hens. And I run back with it across ditch and field, my heart pounding, hugging it half to death, worried am I holding it right or will it peck me maybe and run away squawking and me having to face Mary and all my shame for nothing. And when I get it back to the cottage Mary ties it by one foot with a long bit of string to the leg of the kitchen table and it clucks about the place in and out the door and lays eggs for us and even if it's not true about my daddy coming over The divil the bit of chicken would he get if he did, says Mary, for wouldn't I be foolish indeed to shlaughter such a grand layer?

A big drop of rain fell on my face and a few more splashed on the coffin. Looking up, I saw that heavy black cloud obscured the mainland hills to the east but the sky overhead was clear: we stood at the rim of a passing storm. And I was suddenly aware with all my being of where I was. Seven years earlier, I had stood at the head of my father's coffin on a rainswept hillside above Paisley, so wrecked by sudden grief that I could recall no precise memory of the ceremony. Now I was conscious even of the weight and texture of the cord I held loosely in my hand, linking me with Mary in her coffin and through her with my brother and sister and cousins who had also taken a cord. The few drops of rain had released the tangy smell of the freshly dug earth. Soon we would lay Aunt Mary to rest beside her own aunt, in this grave dug by Mickey Tom, son and cousin, who would lie here himself one day. I heard the hollow drumroll of holy water on the coffinwood and listened as the priest intoned the funeral rites over the grave.

Squinting up the slope into freak winter sunlight, I saw the hillside striped dark with the silhouettes and shadows of these strangers with familiar faces, my first, second and third cousins, my uncles and aunts by blood and by marriage, by highway and byway, by hook and by crook, for better for worse: all the Sweeneys, Cooneys, Corrigans and Fadyens of Achill and, it seemed to me at that moment, the ghosts of all the ancestors we shared. And somewhere in those shadows stood a nine-year-old boy, judging me as I had judged Mickey Tom.

248

I had a powerful sense that I was saying goodbye to this place I had held in my heart all these years. Mary was dead and the cottage would not be the same without her, and its fate was anyway out of my hands. I was free of it now. I felt no bitterness, only the sad harmony of cycles completed, of endings and beginnings. Then I remembered the framed snapshot in my overcoat pocket and I reached in and touched the only inheritance that mattered.

THE END

Acknowledgements

Being more suited to the short sprint than the long haul, I could never have finished this book without the help and support of certain people. I would like to thank:

my agent, David O'Leary, for his patience and good humour;

John Saddler at Anchor Books, who got me to focus on essentials;

the late Liam Hourican, for inspiration;

Pat Hourican and Polli Kaminski, for keeping the faith;

Reggie and Lorna Hoe, whose pleasant home in Brussels was a haven in troubled times;

my sister Margaret and her husband Harry for granting me the seclusion of 'the bothy' in Helensburgh;

all my brothers and sisters: Margaret, Frank, Vincent, Benny and Irene for their willing, if bemused, acquiescence. (What, they must have wondered, is John *doing*?);

my mother for her strength and endurance; my father for his fond and foolish ways. This is their story as much as mine. May they rest in peace.

The Book of the Heathen
Robert Edric

1897. In an isolated station in the Belgian Congo, an Englishman
awaits trial for the murder of a native child, while his friend
attempts to discover the circumstances surrounding the charge. The
world around them is rapidly changing: the horrors of colonial
Africa are becoming known and the flow of its once-fabulous
wealth is drying up.

But there is even more than the death of a child at the heart of
this conflict. There is a secret so dark, so unimaginable, that one
man must be willingly destroyed by his possession of it, and the
other must participate in that destruction.

0 552 99925 3

BLACK SWAN

Back Roads
Tawni O'Dell

THE *NEW YORK TIMES* BESTSELLER

'AN INTENSE STORY OF FAMILY, FRAILTY AND
DYSFUNCTION . . . CAPTIVATINGLY TOLD . . . A
VIVIDLY RENDERED VOYAGE OF PERSONAL
DISCOVERY'
Chicago Tribune

One day Harley Altmyer was 18 and thinking about
making some kind of life. He had a family he loved and
he figured it was time to get a job. Before he has the
chance, his life is a minefield: his father is dead, his
mother in prison for the murder, three younger sisters to
care for, and there's not too much time left over for himself.
Suddenly he has two crummy jobs, a fantasy sex life, big
worries about the kids and a court-appointed therapist.

An intense physical relationship with a woman living
down the road seems to offer a way out, the answer to
his problems. But little can he realise that those
problems are only just beginning . . .

'TENSE, CONFLICTED AND INVOLVING, O'DELL DEFTLY
CAPTURES THE VOICE OF A TEENAGE BOY WHO'S IN
TROUBLE AND FACING PROFOUND CHALLENGES'
New York Times

'HEART-BREAKINGLY HONEST . . . BEAUTIFULLY
WRITTEN . . . A JOURNEY INTO THE WORLD
OF DYSFUNCTIONAL DESPAIR . . . A
REMARKABLE TALE'
San Diego Union

'O'DELL HAS TACKLED THE REAL STUFF OF STORIES
AND SHE'S DONE IT WITH COMPASSION AND A
UNIQUE VOICE . . . A WRITER OF PROMISE'
New York Newsday

'A PAGE-TURNER . . . GRITTY, FUNNY, SEXY'
Chicago Sun-Times

0 552

BLACK SWAN

The Jadu House:
Travels in Anglo-India
Laura Roychowdhury

'INTENSELY PERSONAL, EVOCATIVE, EROTIC'
The Times

Anglo-India is the imaginary and actual terrain in which India and Britain have forged and fought over their relationship for the past two hundred years. A mixed race community, the result of licit and illicit liaisons between the lower classes of British India and Indian women, the story of the Anglo-Indians throws a very different light on the Raj experience from that usually told in memoirs or popular historical accounts.

Once seen as fit only for positions as low-level clerks, prostitutes or film actors, the taint of outcast status still remains even in contemporary India. At the centre of the story is the railway colony at Kharagpur in West Bengal. Designed by the British to be an English village in an Indian landscape, it has become a ghetto where Anglo-Indians protest against the erosion of these two nations' complex and intimate relationship. Through retelling their stories, Laura unsettles our received ideas about the fixed boundaries of race, culture and nationality, and Kharagpur becomes a microcosm of untold, secret colonial histories as well as offering a possible way of re-evaluating the notion of identity.

But this is also the highly personal story of the author herself, who arrived in India a married British woman, only to fall in love with her Bengali research assistant, whom she has since married and whose erotic dialogue frames the beginning of each chapter. It is this union that the author describes as her own original 'sin' and through which she has learnt to understand and, in a sense, become an Anglo-Indian herself.

'A HIGHLY PERSONAL BOOK THAT INTERWEAVES THE MORE INTIMATE MATERIAL OF HER SUBJECTS' LIVES AND HER OWN . . . THOROUGHLY RECOMMENDED. A RIVETING READ, FULL OF FASCINATING STORIES AND INSIGHTS'
Independent

0 552 99913 X

BLACK SWAN

Life Isn't All Ha Ha Hee Hee
Meera Syal

'FUNNY AND SHARP' *Independent*

'A MAGICAL MOSAIC OF FRIENDSHIP, BETRAYAL AND CROSS-CULTURAL INCONGRUITIES. BY TURNS SPICY, HILARIOUS AND SAD, IT UNFOLDS THE TIES THAT BIND YOUNG WOMEN TO THEIR EAST END PUNJABI ROOTS EVEN AS THEY HEAD WEST FOR TRENDY CAREERS, CAFÉ BARS AND SEXUAL FREEDOM' *She*

On a winter morning in London's East End, the locals are confronted with the sight of a white horse skidding through the sooty snow, carrying what looks like a Christmas tree on its back. It turns out to be a man covered in tinsel, with a cartoon-size turban on his head. Entrepreneur Deepak is on his way to get married. As he trudges along, he consoles himself with the thought of marrying Chila, a nice Punjabi girl (a choice which has delighted his surprised parents) does not mean he needs to become his father, grow nostril hair or wear pastel coloured leisure wear.

Life Isn't All Ha Ha Hee Hee is the story of Deepak's bride, the childlike Chila, and her two childhood friends: Sunita, the former activist law student, now an overweight, depressed housewife, and the chic Tanja, who has rejected marriage in favour of a high-powered career in television. A hilarious, thoughful and moving novel about friendship, marriage and betrayal, it focuses on the difficult choices contemporary women have to make, whether or not they happen to be raised in the Asian community.

'EXTREMELY FUNNY, WONDERFULLY INSIGHTFUL . . . A BIG AMBITIOUS BOOK WITH SERIOUS POINTS TO BE MADE ABOUT THE CHOICES WOMEN FACE TODAY . . . SYAL MIXES HER MESSAGE WITH HILARIOUS SET PIECES'
Sunday Express

'A SUPERBLY CRAFTED, PAGE TURNING COMEDY WHICH ISN'T AFRAID TO TACKLE THE BIG SUBJECTS . . . HEARTFELT, HEARTWARMING AND VERY, VERY GOOD'
Mirror

0 552 99952 0

— **BLACK SWAN** —

A SELECTED LIST OF FINE WRITING
AVAILABLE FROM BLACK SWAN

THE PRICES SHOWN BELOW WERE CORRECT AT THE TIME OF GOING TO PRESS. HOWEVER
TRANSWORLD PUBLISHERS RESERVE THE RIGHT TO SHOW NEW RETAIL PRICES ON COVERS
WHICH MAY DIFFER FROM THOSE PREVIOUSLY ADVERTISED IN THE TEXT OR ELSEWHERE.

99916	6	THE NEW CITY	*Stephen Amidon*	£6.99
99946	6	THE ANATOMIST	*Federico Andahazi*	£6.99
99703	X	DOWN UNDER	*Bill Bryson*	£7.99
99979	2	GATES OF EDEN	*Ethan Coen*	£7.99
99926	1	DEAR TOM	*Tom Courtenay*	£7.99
99912	1	BIG SKY	*Gareth Creer*	£6.99
99669	6	ARRANGED MARRIAGE	*Chitra Banerjee Divakaruni*	£6.99
99670	X	THE MISTRESS OF SPICES	*Chitra Banerjee Divakaruni*	£6.99
99767	6	SISTER OF MY HEART	*Chitra Banerjee Divakaruni*	£6.99
99925	3	THE BOOK OF THE HEATHEN	*Robert Edric*	£6.99
99802	8	DON'T WALK IN THE LONG GRASS	*Tenniel Evans*	£6.99
99847	8	WHAT WE DID ON OUR HOLIDAY	*John Harding*	£6.99
99916	4	AMERICAN BY BLOOD	*Andrew Huebner*	£6.99
99796	X	A WIDOW FOR ONE YEAR	*John Irving*	£7.99
14595	5	BETWEEN EXTREMES	*Brian Keenan and John McCarthy*	£7.99
99859		EDDIE'S BASTARD	*William Kowalski*	£6.99
99873	7	SNAKESKIN	*John McCabe*	£6.99
99580	0	CAIRO TRILOGY I: PALACE WALK	*Naguib Mahfouz*	£7.99
14240	9	THE NIGHT LISTENER	*Armistead Maupin*	£6.99
99959	8	BACK ROADS	*Tawni O'Dell*	£6.99
99803	6	THINGS CAN ONLY GET BETTER	*John O'Farrell*	£6.99
99844	3	THE BEST A MAN CAN GET	*John O'Farrell*	£6.99
99913	X	THE JADU HOUSE: Intimate Histories of Anglo-India	*Laura Roychowdhury*	£7.99
99645	9	THE WRONG BOY	*Willy Russell*	£6.99
99750	1	SPEAKING FOR THEMSELVES: The Personal Letters of Winston and Clementine Churchill	*Mary Soames ed.*	£15.00
99952	0	LIFE ISN'T ALL HA HA HEE HEE	*Meera Syal*	£6.99

All Transworld titles are available by post from:

Bookpost, PO Box 29, Douglas, Isle of Man, IM99 1BQ

Credit cards accepted. Please telephone 01624 836000,
fax 01624 837033, Internet http://www.bookpost.co.uk
or e-mail: bookshop@enterprise.net for details

Free postage and packing in the UK. Overseas customers:
allow £1 per book (paperbacks) and £3 per book (hardbacks)